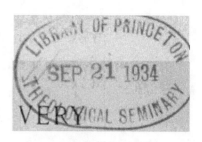

POEMS BY JONES VERY

An Introductory Memoir

BY

WILLIAM P. ANDREWS

And all their motions upward be,
And ever as they mount, like larks they sing.
The note is sad, yet music for a king.
GEORGE HERBERT

BOSTON
HOUGHTON, MIFFLIN AND COMPANY
New York: 11 East Seventeenth Street
The Riverside Press, Cambridge
1883

Inscribed

To the Beloved Memory of the Author's dear Brother,

WASHINGTON VERY.

Preface.

———♦———

THE first edition of Mr. Very's writings was prepared by Mr. Emerson, and published at his request by Messrs. Little & Brown, at Boston in 1839, under the title of "Essays and Poems." It was long since exhausted, though never reprinted, and consisted of three essays in prose and something less than half of the poetical pieces here given.

The essays received high praise from eminent sources, though it is thought best not to include them in the present collection of the poetry, whose pure, bird-like note of unpremeditated song was at that time, if not still, a unique production here; and stood (as Mr. Dana remarked of it) quite "apart" in American literature. It was hailed with delight by the leading literary men then on this side of the Atlantic (*vide* Memoir, pp. 9–11), whose feeling for this genuine, underived voice of New England piety finds

expression, it is hoped, in the lines which Mr.
Very's literary friends have desired should stand
as an introduction to this collection of his poetry.

If the verse alluded to seems to overestimate
the value of that poetry, it is to be remembered
that it applies only to the condition of poetical
literature in this country half a century ago;
and it is to be noted that it understates the impression which Mr. Very's remarkable originality
and fervor of pure devotion made upon his contemporaries.

The present collection has been arranged with
a view of showing the development of the Author's religious idea connectedly; and has been
divided into such groupings and sequences as the
subject naturally assumes by headings, taken
from his writings, which serve to denote the
character of the group so inclosed. Though not
including all the verse even produced during the
period of Mr. Very's remarkable exaltation, it
presents throughout a closely connected sequence
of thought, and a complete picture of a deep and
unusual religious experience, that colors all of
the writer's work; some of which, of earlier and
later origin, is included for general literary
reasons.

Into it all he poured his inmost soul; whose history is here written with an intensity which varied with the writer's spiritual and mental condition. All of Mr. Very's verse is absolutely composed without a thought of literary form, — though it has an unstudied grace of its own, — and with a spontaneity which is almost as rare as it is conceded to be admirable in literary art.

WM. P. ANDREWS.

SALEM, MASS., *February*, 1883.

Contents.

x   *CONTENTS.*

CONTENTS.

xii CONTENTS.

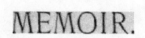

MEMOIR.

"*An extra-mundane character with reference to this globe, and though not a native of the moon, not made of the dust of this planet.*" — COWPER.

MEMOIR.

JONES VERY, the poet, was born at Salem, on Massachusetts Bay, on the 28th of August, 1813. He was the eldest of six children, two of whom died in infancy. His brother, the Rev. Washington Very, who died in early manhood, and Miss L. L. A. Very, the younger of his two sisters, who still survive him, exhibited also a decided talent for versification, which they seem to have inherited from their parents, both of whom were fond of composing verses, and sometimes included them in their letters to the children.

Mr. Very's father, "Capt." Jones Very, a son of "Capt." Isaac Very of Spencer, Mass., and his third wife Rachel (Jones) Very, was, like his father before him, a shipmaster, and followed the sea from early life. He was one of the shipmasters whose intelligence and gentlemanly bearing made the name of New England honored on all seas. Married early in life to his cousin, Lydia Very of Salem, he seems to have been a highly respected and useful citizen, and was soon given command of a vessel. He made many successful voyages, on the last two of which, in

1823 to Cronstadt, and in 1824 to New Orleans,
he was accompanied by his son Jones, then a boy
of nine.[1]

While in New Orleans young Jones was sent
to school, and on his return to Salem he went

---

[1] By the following genealogical note, for which we are indebted
to the researches of Dr. Henry Wheatland, President of the Essex
Institute in Salem, in the publications of which Society it was first
printed, it appears that the family is traced back to *Bridget Very*,[1]
who came from England with her two sons and a daughter, and
was a member of the First Church in Salem in 1648. She and
her son Samuel[2] lived on the north side of Cedar Pond, near the
Danvers almshouse, where they owned a large tract of land, and
where her descendants resided for a century or more. Many of
them removed to Salem and became shipmasters.

Samuel Very,[2] born in England about 1619, married Alice, daughter of John Woodis, Woodhouse or Woodice, had:

Benjamin Very,[3] married Jemima, daughter of Joseph Newhall
of Lynn; had:

Isaac Very,[4] born July 30, 1715; married Elizabeth Giles in 1736;
a corporal under Colonel Ichabod Plaisted in 1756; died at Sandy
Hook in the army, 1778; had sons Isaac and Samuel.

Samuel Very,[5] born in Salem, December 10, 1755; married, in
1776, Hannah Putney. She died February 4, 1799. He was a master and owner of a vessel, but kept a store many years in Salem at
the corner of Essex and Boston streets; died in 1824, aged 69; had:
Lydia,[6] born June 14, 1792; married her cousin, Jones Very, and was
the mother of the subject of this sketch.

Isaac Very,[5] born in Salem, 1745; married, for his third wife,
Rachel Jones of Charlton. He resided some years in Charlton and
Spencer, the later part of his life in Salem; was master of a vessel
and an officer of the customs, Salem. He died in 1831, aged 86;
had:

Jones Very,[6] the father of the poet, born in Spencer, Mass., November 17, 1790, and followed the seas from early life. As a shipmaster he sailed in the employ of the Hon. William Gray from 1817
to 1821, in the brig Concord; from 1821 to September, 1824, in the
barque Aurelia. He married his cousin, Lydia Very, above men-
tioned. He resided at the corner of Essex and Boston streets in
Salem. He died December 22, 1824.

back to the Public Grammar School, where he was remarked as a shy, modest lad, who took little part in the boyish sports of his fellows. This fact, and a certain diffidence and reserve of manner, tended to limit the number of his school intimates, though he was respected and beloved by all who came in contact with him.

In December, 1824, his father died, and his mother, a woman of much decision of character, was left to bring up her young family alone. To her the poet was indebted for his ardent love of flowers, and his graceful lines, entitled "My Mother's Voice," show the warm affection and harmonious relation that existed between them. Mrs. Very was inclined to be skeptical of the shallower religious pretensions and conventions, but reverenced her son's lofty self-abnegation; and in the height of his religious ecstasy she shielded him from much annoyance incident to the reception of his exalted views of human duty and conduct, — opinions that shocked the serene contentment of the conventional clergymen and respectable pillars of the churches; who declared that Very and his friend Emerson were dangerous persons, and that they should be indicted, or at least incarcerated in an asylum for the insane.

Young Very was a devoted student, and his great desire was to lead a literary life, and to go, as he expressed it, "to the depths of literature." He was unusually mature for his age, and passed

the larger part of his time in study, but the care
of his father's family had devolved upon him,
and when he was fourteen years old he went into
an auction room in Salem as errand and store
boy. He as conscientiously discharged these new
and distasteful duties as he did the more con-
genial tasks of the school-room ; but occupied all
his well-earned moments of leisure in perfecting
his education. He seized with avidity on all
books that passed through his employer's hands,
and purchased such as his slender means would
allow. In exchange for a rare copy of Shakespeare which he procured in this way, he obtained from a student the books necessary to fit
him for college, and with the kindly assistance of
Mr. J. Fox Worcester, a gentleman engaged in
preparing young men for the university, he
fitted himself to become a tutor in a private Latin
school in Salem, then presided over by Mr.
Henry K. Oliver. He assisted Mr. Oliver in
preparing boys for entrance in the freshman
class, and pursued the studies of the first col-
legiate year meantime with that gentleman. In
1834 an uncle of young Very furnished what
pecuniary aid he needed, and he entered Harvard College, Cambridge, Mass., in the last term
of the sophomore year. He graduated in 1836
with the second honors (the first being given to
a scholar of the same rank who had pursued the
entire course within the university), and was ap-

pointed a tutor in Greek, studying Theology at
the same time in the Divinity School.

In college, as in school, he was too sedate to
be widely and generally popular, but all who
knew him reverenced the lofty purity of his
character, and he soon gathered around him a
small circle of warmly attached friends. He was
sensitive and reserved, but the cordiality of his
tone and the sweet naturalness of his smile of
welcome at once attracted whoever made his
acquaintance, though the uniform gravity of his
daily walk and conversation prevented the many
from approaching him as an intimate.

He diligently followed his studies in the Divinity School, but found time to devote more
than the then usual attention to his pupils in the
Greek class.

He has since been spoken of, by those under
his charge, as an ideal instructor; "one who
fairly breathed the spirit of the Greek language
and its literature, surrounding the study with a
charm which," his pupils declare, "vanished from
Harvard with him." He, however, disclaimed
any especial merit as an instructor, saying, in
answer to a compliment on his success, that he
"only let the Greek grow." He visited the
students in their rooms also, and asked them to
walk with him; talking meanwhile of the highest
spiritual themes, but in a tone so devout and so
far removed from cant as to command the at-

tention of even the most thoughtless ; a striking
proof of his power.   Forty-four years afterward
the hilarities of a class supper were suspended,
that each member present might bear loving
testimony to his individual sense of obligation to
Mr. Very's instruction and the force of his personal influence.

The verses which flowed from his pen often
first appeared on the backs of the young men's
Greek exercises as incentives toward a nobler
life; and his best literary work was produced at
this time (1836–38).   His intense application,
and the excitement of his exalted spiritual condition proved too much for his health, and in
1838 he retired to Salem in search of needed
rest.

There the stream of poetry flowed on uninter-
ruptedly, and it is a noticeable fact that all his
more important work was produced in this spon-
taneous, unstudied way.   He, with Milton, regarded its accomplishment as lying not with him,
"but in a Power above him;" as proceeding
directly from what Milton speaks of, in alluding
to his own great projected work, as "that Eternal Spirit, who can enrich with all utterance and
knowledge, and sends out his seraphim with the
hallowed fire of his altar, to touch and purify the
lips of whom He pleases."

He had become intensely interested in the subject of religion, and was inclined to carry this

Miltonic view of inspiration to its last results. He was therefore thought by many persons to be insane, but Rev. Dr. Clarke, who saw him at this time, declared it to be a case of "MONO-SANIA rather than *mono-mania;*" and Mr. Emerson wrote that he regarded him as "profoundly sane," and "*wished the whole world were as mad as he.*" Dr. Clarke said he failed to find evidence of derangement, and "saw only the workings of a mind absorbed in the loftiest contemplations of religious truth, and which utterly disregarded all which did not come into that high sphere of thought." He said: "Mr. Very's views in regard to religion were not different from those heretofore advocated by many pure and earnestly religious persons. He maintains, as did Fénelon, Mme. Guion, and others, that all sin consists in self-will, all holiness in unconditional surrender of our own will to the will of God. He believes that one whose object is not to do his own will in anything, but constantly to obey God, is led by Him, and taught of Him in all things. He is a son of God as Christ was THE SON, because he always did the things which pleased his Father."

Mr. Very said that every man would attain to this when he made the final sacrifice in filial obedience; and he believed himself to have done so.

Miss E. P. Peabody, who was then intimate with both Mr. Very and Rev. Dr. Channing, reports the latter as being "immensely impressed and touched with his union of gentleness and modesty, and yet complete sense of his word being the utterance of the Holy Spirit;" and as saying that "he had not lost his reason, but only held his senses, his lower faculties in abeyance." "Men in general," said Dr. Channing, "have lost or never found this higher mind, their insanity is profound, Mr. Very's is only superficial. To hear him talk was like looking into the purely spiritual world, into truth itself. He had nothing of self-exaggeration, but seemed to have attained self-annihilation and become an oracle of God." Dr. Channing repeated that he had "not lost his reason," and quoted some of his sayings, identical with many parts of his sonnets, as proofs of the "iron sequence of his thought." "Wells of thought, clear and pellucid, and coming up from profound depths," Dr. Clarke had called them in the notice of Mr. Very before quoted from; and Hawthorne has embalmed them in the album of his "Virtuoso's Collection," as the utterances of "a poet whose voice is scarcely heard among us as yet by reason of its depth." Referring to an interview in which Very had delivered his mission to him, Hawthorne speaks of his (Very's) limitations as arising from want of a sense of the ludicrous; but regarded his views as sanctified by his real piety and goodness. He added, however, that "he had better

remain as he is — one organ in the world of im-
personal spirit — at least as long as he can write
such good sonnets." Our elder poet, Mr. Richard
H. Dana, spoke of them in one of his friendly
notes to Mr. Very, as "so deeply and poetically
thoughtful; so true in language, so complete as
a whole." He also wrote to his other poet
friend, Mr. Bryant, that he regarded them as
"standing apart here in those qualities;" and
with this judgment Mr. Bryant cordially agreed;
often commenting upon their "extraordinary
grace and originality," and formally pronouncing
them "among the finest in the language."

Mr. R. W. Emerson hailed them as "bearing
the unquestionable stamp of grandeur." "They
are," he says, "the breathings of a certain en-
tranced devotion; as sincere a litany as the Hebrew songs of David or Isaiah, and only less
than they, because they are indebted to the
Hebrew Muse for their tone and genius. They
have the sublime unity of the Decalogue or the
Code of Menu; and if as monotonous, yet are
they almost as pure as the sounds of surrounding
Nature." Mr. George William Curtis has lately
remarked, "it is plain that they are gems of
purest ray serene;" and another competent
critic has happily characterized them as "a
soul's history written with a pen of light." As
pure literature they are highly interesting, amid
the present flood of secondary and derived work;

and, as Goethe said of another genuine poet of a
single note: "the true test of all literary greatness dwells with him, that the more intimately
you know him, the more you love and admire
him."

Mr. Very regarded these sonnets as containing
a "message" which had been "given him" to
deliver; for he was infinitely modest about his
own part in their production, and thought himself but a reed through which the Spirit might
breathe a music of its own. It was a perfectly
natural consequence, he believed, of his submis-
sion to the Divine Will; and would always follow if man offered no selfish obstruction to the
movement of that Holy Spirit, ever striving to
manifest itself in the human soul.

In this earlier period of his most remarkable
production, during the years 1837–38 and '39,
these verses poured forth from him with extraordinary rapidity, and were penciled down as
they "came" to him, on a great sheet of paper
which he had folded to pages of small note size.
Miss Peabody says they were produced at the
rate of one or two a day. When the sheet was
full Mr. Very brought it to her, and she trans-
mitted it to Mr. Emerson at Concord, who afterward printed these verses with others, which Mr.
Very himself gave him, substantially unaltered.

Mr. Emerson says in his private journal, of
Very: "Our Saint was very unwilling to allow

correction " (of his verses), "but his friend said, I supposed you were too high in your thought to mind such trifles." He replied, "I value these verses not because they are *mine*, but because they are *not*."

Mr. Emerson's notes on Mr. Very, made in his journals of the time, are so valuable as exhibiting the character of Mr. Very's thought, that they may well be given here as originally jotted down. The first entry occurs under date of October 26, 1838, and it and the others, made apparently about the same time, are as follows:

Jones Very came hither two days since. His position accuses society as much as society names that false and morbid. And much of his discourse concerning society, church, and college was absolutely just.

He says it is with him a day of hate: that he discerns the bad element in every person whom he meets, which repels him: he even shrinks a little to give the hand, that sign of receiving. The institutions, the cities which men have built the world over, look to him like a huge ink-blot. His only guard in going to see men is, that he goes to do them good, else they would injure him spiritually. He lives in the sight that He who made him, made the things he sees. He would as soon embrace a black Egyptian mummy as Socrates. He would obey, — obey. He is not disposed to attack religions or charities, though false. The bruisëd reed he would not break, smoking flax not quench.

He answered L., " your thought speaks there, and not your life; " and he is very sensible of interference in thought and act. A very accurate discernment of spirits belongs to his state, and he detects at once the presence of an alien element, though he cannot tell whence, how, or whereto it is.

He thinks me covetous in my hold of truth, of seeing truth separate, and of receiving or taking it, instead of merely obeying. The will is to him all; — as to me, after my own showing, truth. He is sensible in one of a little colder air than that he breathes. He says, " You do not disobey because you do the wrong act, but you do the wrong act because you first disobey. And you do not obey because you do the good action, but you do the good action because you first obey."

He has nothing to do with time, because he obeys. A man who is busy has no time, he does not recognize that element. A man who is idle says he does not know what to do with his time. Obedience is in eternity.

He says it is the necessity of the Spirit to speak with authority.

He had the manners of a man, — one, that is, to whom life was more than meat. He felt it, he said, an honor to wash his face, being, as it was, the temple of the Spirit.

I ought not to omit to record the astonishment which seized all the company when our brave Saint the other day fronted the presiding Preacher. The Preacher began to tower and dogmatize with many words. Then I foresaw that his doom was fixed; and, as soon as he had ceased speaking, the Saint set him right, and blew away all his words in an instant, —unhorsed him, I may say, and tumbled him along the ground in utter dismay, like my angel of Heliodorus; never was discomfiture more complete. In tones of genuine pathos, he bid him wonder at the Love which suffered him to speak there in his chair of things he knew nothing of; one might expect to see the book taken from his hands and him thrust out of the room, and yet he was allowed to sit and talk, whilst every word he spoke was a step of departure from the truth; and of this he commanded himself to bear witness.

In the woods, he said to me, " One might forget here that the world was desert and empty, and all the people wicked."

When he is in the room with other persons, speech stops, as if there were a corpse in the apartment.

At Walden Pond, when the water was much disturbed by the wind, he said : " See how each wave rises from the midst with an original force, at the same time that it partakes of an original movement."

In our walk Jones Very said that he had been to Cambridge and that he had there found his brother in his chamber reading Livy. "I asked him," he continued, "if the Romans were masters of the world? My brother said they had been ; I told him they were still. Then I went into the room of a senior, who lived opposite, and found him writing a theme; I asked him what was his subject? and he said, Cicero's Vanity; I asked him if the Romans were masters of the world. He said they had been; I told him they were still. This was in the garret of Mr. Ware's house where my brother's room was.

Then I went down into Mr. Ware's study, and found him reading Bishop Butler, and I asked him if the Romans were masters of the world? He said they had been; I told him they were still."

What led him to study Shakespeare was the fact that all young men say, Shakespeare was no saint — yet see what Genius. He wished to solve that problem. When he was asked, "What was the difference between wisdom and genius? he replied: "Wisdom was of God," — but he had left genius, and could not speak of it. He was pressed further, and said, "Genius was the decay of Wisdom." He added: "To the preëxistent Shakespeare, Wisdom was offered; but he did not accept it, and so he died away into Genius. When his Vineyard was given him, God looked that he should bring forth grapes, but he brought forth sour grapes." "But," said the interrogator, "My grapes tasted sweet." He replied: "That was because you knew not the sweet. All things are sweet, until there comes a sweeter."

When Jones Very was in Concord, he had said to me: "I always felt when I heard you speak, or read your writings, that you saw the truth better than others; yet I felt that your spirit was not quite right. It was as if a vein of colder air blew across me." He seemed to expect from me, — once especially in Walden wood, — a full acknowledgment of his mission, and a participation in the same. Seeing this, I asked him if he did not see that my thoughts and my position were constitutional, that it would be false and impossible for me to say his things or try to occupy his ground as for him to usurp mine? After some frank and full explanation he conceded this. When I met

him afterwards, one evening at my lecture in Boston,
I invited him to go home to Mr. A.'s with me and
sleep; which he did. He slept in the room adjoining
mine. Early next day, in the gray dawn, he came
into my room, and talked whilst I dressed. He
said: "When I was in Concord, I tried to say you
were also right; but the Spirit said you were not
right. It is just as if I should say, It is not morning,
but the Morning says, It is the Morning."

His words were loaded with his fact. What he
said, he held, was not personal to him, was no more
disputable than the shining of yonder sun, or the
blowing of this south wind.

At the McLean Asylum the patients severally
thanked him when he came away, and told him that
he had been of great service to them.

Jones Very is gone into the multitude as solitary
as Jesus. In dismissing him, I seem to have discharged an arrow into the heart of Society. Wher-
ever that young enthusiast goes, he will astonish and
disconcert men by dividing for them the cloud that
covers the gulf in man.

The astonishment in the minds of the staid
citizens of Salem was already apparent, and as
his enthusiasm increased, he quickly proceeded
to disconcert the somewhat formal clergymen of
that peaceful city, by dividing for them the cloud
which covered the gulf between the usual conventional observance of religious forms and the
tremendous demands involved in a literal and
unhesitating acceptance of the precepts of Christ
and the Christian example. He finally called on

the different members of the profession and
offered to pray with them, that they too might
submit themselves wholly to the Divine Will and
be baptized with the Holy Ghost. He was generally received with courtesy and consideration;
but this view of the clerical duty was rather too
much for the good-nature of some of the brethren, and they demanded that Mr. Very be shut
up in an insane asylum. His mother, however,
stood between him and any forcible removal,
though he put himself for a while under the care
of Dr. Bell at the Asylum in Somerville, who
shortly sent him home, freed from physical ex-
haustion and the excitement incident to the vi-
olent opposition his fearless "bearing of testimony" had naturally enough aroused.

While under Dr. Bell's care he finished the
paper on Shakespeare, included in the collection
made by Mr. Emerson, together with the other
admirable papers on Hamlet and on Epic Poetry.
This latter he had delivered in Salem the winter
before as a lecture, and Miss Peabody was so
deeply impressed with its unusual merit that she
wrote at once to Mr. Emerson, suggesting his
inviting Mr. Very to lecture in Concord, and the
advisability of his making the acquaintance of
this remarkable young man. This Mr. Emerson
did, and wrote to Miss Peabody under date of
April 5, 1838: —

"But what I write for is to thank again your sa-

gacity that detects such wise men as Mr. Very, from
whose conversation and lecture I have had a true
and high satisfaction. I heartily congratulate myself on being, as it were, anew in such company."

Several times in the course of this year Mr.
Emerson writes to Miss Peabody of the satisfaction he has had in visits from Mr. Very, and in
November he writes to Mr. Very thanking him
for lectures and sonnets which he "loves," and
has had copied, and reads "to all who have ears
to hear." "Do not," Mr. Emerson adds, "Do
not, I beg of you, let a whisper or a sigh of the
Muse go unattended to, or unrecorded. The
sentiment which inspires your poetry is so deep
and true, and the expression so simple, that I am
sure you will find your audience very large."

In the following June Mr. Emerson writes to
Miss Peabody : —•

"I cannot persuade Mr. Very to remain with me
another day. He says he is not permitted, and no
assurances that his retirement shall be secured are
of any avail. He has been serene, intelligent, and
true in all the conversation I have had with him.
He gives me pleasure and much relief, after all I had
heard concerning him."

Mr. Emerson adds he shall himself go to
town and attend to the publication of Mr. Very's
book.

From Mr. Very's letters of this period to Mr.
Emerson we can see how truly his verses reflect

his mental condition at that time. He writes to Mr. Emerson in September, 1838 : —

"I am glad at last to be able to transmit what has been told me of Shakespeare — 't is but the faint echo of that which speaks to you now. . . . You hear not mine own words, but the teachings of the Holy Ghost. . . . My friend, I tell you these things as they are told me, and hope soon for a day or two of leisure, when I may speak to you face to face as I now write."

In November of the same year he writes : —

"I was glad to hear that my stay with you was improving, and that you love that which is spoken by the Word. If you love it aright, in the spirit of obedience, it shall be unto *you* given to hear and speak of the Father in Christ. . . . You must pass out of that world in which you are, naked (that is, willess) as you came in. Then shall you have a *new* will born of the Spirit, and when this also is submitted to the Father's you shall be one with Him; that is, be prepared to see Him as a spirit. Every scribe instructed in the Kingdom shall bring forth, as a householder, new and old; that is, he himself shall hear the word of the Father, and anew interpret for men the old. But so far have the false Christs failed in this life, that they do not even claim to hear of themselves the Word, and vainly attempt to bring forth that once spoken."

He sends some poems of his own Mr. Emerson has asked for, and says : —

"I was wearied much by a few days' stay in Cambridge, but am now as if with you again and well; waiting for that daily direction which is a path unseen through the world and its visible evils; — in which that we all may walk forever and ever I pray always."

Again he writes, with more poems : —

"I send you these by letter that they may come earlier to hand. I hardly dared to write *them*, and that will excuse me from a letter. They are the true letter, as I am true. There is more joy and freedom as I advance, yet still I long to be clothed upon with my house from heaven. In you, too, may more of the old pass away, and the new and abiding be more and more felt. This I pray forever, as

"I am   J. VERY."

Among Mr. Emerson's papers were also some formal epistles of Mr. Very's, setting forth his ideas more at length. In one, on the subject of Prayer, he says : —

"He who is born" [he means by this, born anew into this spirit of utter self-abnegation] "is alone said by God, or in Scripture language, to *deny* himself. This is prayer! And by it you show that you love the brethren, because you cannot love more than this, that you accomplish the entire denial of the life you have attained unto by being born. . . . This is prayer, in sincerity *ever* to love your neighbor as yourself. It [that is, the new birth in the Spirit] has not really begun till then. When you, who are unborn, are using words to which you give that name, there is no agency at work benefiting those for whom you thus speak. . . . It is your words which are proceeding from your inward growth or backwardness that convey this influence to others. Use what language you will, you can never *say* anything but what you *are*. Whoever lives better than you knows what you are really saying, whatever the sounds of your lips. The Spirit will always work, whether it be good, or whether it be evil."

Again he says, in the epistle on " Miracles:"—

" One may forward you who is living the same life, or passing toward the same life as yourself; he *alone* can raise you, or act upon you with a power different from your own, who *lives* that other life, and has already passed before you into it. . . . As in a glass face answers to face, so will my heart then answer to yours. Now you see me, if sight it may be called, externally, with an unchanged spirit; then face to face. Now you make me what I am to you; then you shall see me as I AM ; for you yourself will be made like unto me. Then shall you know that it was *I* who called you forth from the grave ; it was *I* who raised you from the bed of sickness; and you will arise and minister unto *me.*"

It is not to be wondered at that gentlemen engaged in plodding along pleasant ministerial highways did not relish this sort of light in their quiet studies of a Monday morning, and declared the presumptuous young person to be hopelessly insane, and in league with the Arch Enemy.

Mr. Very's own life as a minister, when he recovered his health, and, in 1843, was licensed

to preach by the Cambridge Association of
Ministers, was never a "popular" success; but
after his death the truth of what he here says of
the strength of this unseen influence was forcibly
illustrated in many unsought testimonials to the
inspiration his life had been to all sorts and con-
ditions of men. "To have walked with Very,"
said a brother clergyman, "was truly to have
walked with God." So filled was his spirit with
the immanence of the encircling Power Divine.
"I told my people," said a singularly eloquent
preacher, "that to see Very for half an hour in
my pulpit, and know that such a man existed in
the world, was a far greater sermon than any
ever preached to them from the lips of an ora-
tor." And a sportsman remarked to the writer:
"I don't set up to be a religious man; but you
could n't meet Very in the fields without feeling
better for it somehow." It is a noticeable fact
that this feeling for Mr. Very knew no bounds
of sect, or of intellectual attainment. It was
indeed an "o'erflowing well," of whose cool
waters all men gladly drank, and "*owned its
source Divine.*"

"He was as good," said his life-long friend,
the Rev. Robert C. Waterston, "as goodness itself, true as truth. With his knowledge and
wisdom, he was as simple as a child, transparent,
artless. He was the extremest possible distance
from pomposity or pretension. When he be-

lieved that the poetry, which came to him like the breath of heaven, did actually come from Heaven, it was so naturally and simply said, that you felt it was his profoundest conviction. He believed fully and intensely that the Lord of Life gave it to him. It was a sacred idea, a Divine Reality."

This nearness of the Divine Presence was to Mr. Very the great fact of life. He felt it to be so intensely real and vital that he was inexpressibly grieved, as he looked around among his fellows for men who *thus* "walked with God," to find how much alone he stood; and he breaks out into a wail of lamentation that men are dead to the glory round them, and in a bondage worse than slavery. He "cannot tell the sorrows that he feels" for his brethren dying in the hideous darkness of a prison, when they should be working with and enjoying with the Father.

His own intense, contemplative piety had lifted him out of what he regarded as "the grave" of the senses, above the world, into that condition of "inward peace, the sweet patience" which the Buddhist calls Nirvâna. In the height of his ecstasy he would sit for hours wrapt in thought and gazing off into the Infinite. Like the saintly Buddhs, he seemed long since to have slain the "love of self, false faith, and doubt," and, conqueror over "the love of life on earth, desire for heaven, self-praise, error, and pride," he had become

" As one who stands on yonder snowy horn,
  Having naught o'er him but the boundless blue,
For, these sins being slain, the man had come
  Nirvâna's verge unto."

The considerate and tender manner in which
everything was done for Mr. Very removed this
undue exhilaration under which he was acting,
and restored the ordinary balance of his faculties.
Yet he retained to the last, though he ceased
to go about promulgating it, his great idea:
that every man who made the complete sacrifice
of self necessary to the identification with, the
hiding in Christ, would become the voice of the
Holy Ghost. He believed himself to have done
so. He, however, never assumed the rôle of a
proselyter. His whole duty was to utter the
words " given " him ; he was not responsible for
their effect or non-effect on others. He printed
his verses in the columns of the local papers published in his native town ; but was in no hurry to
get them before the world. As we have seen, he
did not feel at liberty even to correct them for
the press, but allowed Mr. Emerson's repeated
solicitation to prevail, in want of any direct " leading " to publish them himself; and the first and,
except the present, the only collection of Mr.
Very's writings — fifty sonnets in the Shakespear-
ean form, a few lyrics, and three prose essays
— accordingly appeared, at the request of Mr.
Emerson, from the house of Messrs. Little &
Brown in 1839.

That edition was never reprinted, though it was long since exhausted; and among Mr. Very's letters many requests from Mr. Dana and other friends were found for more copies, for which they had searched the bookstores in vain.

The present collection has been compiled with a view of showing the history of this remarkable spiritual experience connectedly; and the selections in this volume are, therefore, mainly such as seem moved by this Divine afflatus, this unique exaltation of spirit, which made so profound an impression upon his contemporaries. This lasted, however, only during the limited period described (*i. e.* 1838 and parts of 1837–39), though he continued to the end of his life to write and print new verses as before. Some of these later productions are included in the present volume, and all have the same outward excellence of form which marked his earlier, more inspired measures, though they are quite unimpassioned, and simple to a degree. Yet in all that he has done, — however unattractive it may prove to the purely literary critic, — we find the same delicate aroma of his gentle and gracious spirit, and it is always an unconscious utterance of devout and pure aspiration.

After this excessive exhilaration had subsided into the serene calm of his later existence, he lived on very quietly in the family home with his sisters, — his mother and brother having died many

years before his own death. He was not married,
and seems to have found his domestic happiness
in the original family circle. Occasionally he
would go from home for a short time to supply
some Unitarian pulpit, but he was not perma-
nently settled, and he remained, as he says, "a
laborer but in heart." That labor was, however,
so sincere, that his influence, as we have seen,
was much deeper and more wide-spread than that
of many shepherds whose sheep are gathered
together into close-barred and visible folds. He
was always the still, small voice apart from the
bustle of humanity, and — but that his intense
love of Nature and ever-present sense of Deity
peopled the loneliest solitudes with his friends —
his life must have been somewhat monotonous
and dreary. That he did at times feel the want
of a vital human sympathy near at hand, is evi-
dent from a letter to his friend Mr. Waterston,
written in 1868, in which he says : —

" Those were indeed pleasant and precious days,
when we enjoyed so much each other's companionship
at Cambridge. Then thoughts and feelings were
freely interchanged and our lives were blended in
one. There is nothing," he adds, " which we miss
more in our manhood than that delightful communion which we enjoyed with early friends. Such an
intercourse and communion it is we are toiling all
our lives to find, — not perhaps to be renewed here,
but which we hope is reserved to continue forever in
heaven."

His life was, indeed, peculiarly uneventful; though never that of an intentional recluse. His mornings were spent in study and a somewhat general course of scientific and literary reading; and his afternoons in rambles over the rocky hills and through the mossy dells of the wild pasture land surrounding the upper portion of his native city. These wanderings were generally unaccompanied; for, though all sorts of men liked to walk with him, his contemplative, introspective habit of mind kept him rather apart from his fellows; albeit every one was sure of the kindliest welcome, from the little boys, with whom he was indeed "a child again," to the gravest of his clerical brethren. His love of Nature was a passion "deeper far than strength of words can tell;" or rather it was more truly a devotion, since it was the Divinity behind her outward beauty which made her all in all to him, and attuned his soul in accord with her inmost harmonies. He would return from these rambles and put into manuscript the words there "given" him, the bird-like strains of his wholly unpremeditated art; and if they were not, as he thought them, the utterances of the Holy Ghost, they certainly were the melodies of Nature.

Though at times somewhat disheartened and inclined to lament the blindness of mankind, he in the end is always hopeful and cheerful, because always filled with unswerving faith and childlike trust. So he went about his daily routine, of reading alike from books and from nature of the Father's wonders and goodness ; composing verses, as Wordsworth did, out of doors ; preaching when asked to, and always striving to exert in an unobtrusive way an influence for good. However careless, light-hearted, or bad-hearted might be those about him, he greeted them all with the same grave courtesy and benign, sweet smile; and always invisibly clothed in his spotless singing-robes, wandered alike with God through the busy market-place or over the loved hill-side.

His brother poet and clergyman, the Rev. Charles T. Brooks, — also a Salem boy, — speaks of Mr. Very's " peculiarly sweet smile, lighting up that face so singularly expressive of saintly simplicity and unselfish translucency of soul," and says " he recalled the ideal preacher in the 'Task ;' or Uhland's 'Country Parson.'" Izaak Walton's description of saintly George Herbert exactly pictures Mr. Very as he appeared in later life.[1] " He was," says Walton, " for his person, of a stature inclining towards tallness ; his body was very straight, and so far from being

---

[1] In a note on a letter of Emerson's to Carlyle (*Correspondence*, vol. i. p. 333), accompanying a copy of Very's *Essays and Poems*, which Emerson requests Carlyle to show to Sterling " and ask him if they have not a grandeur," Mr. Charles Eliot Norton observes: "A little volume, the work of an exquisite spirit. Some of the poems it contains are as if written by a George Herbert who had studied Shakespeare, read Wordsworth, and lived in America."

cumbered with too much flesh, that he was lean
to an extremity. His aspect was cheerful, and
his speech and motion did both declare him a
gentleman; for they were all so meek and oblig-
ing, that they purchased love and respect from
all that knew him."

There *was* something in his personal appear-
ance and manner, as well as in the inspired ca-
dences of his Saxon verse, which always reminded
one of a more gracious and tranquil past. Not
that he was more conservative in his dress than
many of his contemporaries in the quiet old town
in which he lived and died; yet, when one saw
the tall, slight figure outlined against a glowing
twilight sky, gazing off from some of the craggy
hill-tops over which he loved to ramble; or perhaps disappearing down a distant valley mellowed
with the golden afternoon sunlight, —

"Rapt, twirling in his hand a withered spray,
And waiting for the spark from heaven to fall,"

it seemed, indeed, as if a gentle presence had
wandered here, from another world than ours.

"To look at him, to know him," said his friend
and admirer, Mr. E. A. Silsbee, "was to see
Genius. He moved in Salem like Dante among
the Florentines: a man who had seen God; . . .
and drew his inspiration from the Spirit itself,
far away in the soul, where no ambition comes,
but only lowliness, humility, and seeking."

On the 8th of May, Anno Domini 1880, in the home where so much of his simple existence had been passed, his weary eyes closed for the last time in sleep, and he fully entered that "New Birth" which he had long since sung in some of his noblest numbers.

"The flower that on the lovely hill-side grows"

in vain expects him there when Spring has given its bloom again; but many a tree and bush his wanderings know, and, as the sweet birds sing on, their spirit-songs,

"And e'en the clouds and silent stars of heaven"

repeat his solemn story.

WILLIAM P. ANDREWS.

SALEM, MASS., *March*, 1883.

POEMS.

JONES VERY.

We thought: the morning birds have ceased to sing,
  We hear but songs from out a gilded cage;
When to our August noon a breath of Spring
  Brought us a strain from out another age;
The sultry airs no longer round us blew,
  The whole wide earth took on a living green,
Flowers bloomed again where erst in Spring they grew,
  And beckoned where but sun-dried heath had been.

O Saint and Poet! on our world-worn time,
  Thy waiting spirit breathed that quick'ning lay;
Thy rapt soul heard the harmonies sublime,
  And sang the music of a loftier day;
The Soul of all things in thy pulses stirred,
And soared in praises like the morning bird.
                                    W. P. A.

The Call.

POEMS.

The Tent.

THOU springest from the ground, and may not I
From Him who spreads thy branches high and
　　　wide;
And from the scorching sun and stormy sky
May I not too with friendly shelter hide?
There is no shade like thine to shield the poor
From the hot scorching words that meet the ear;
The snowy, frozen flakes they must endure
Of those whose hearts have never shed a tear;
Yet He who shoots thy leafy fabric high,
Shall in my verse spread wide a tempering screen,
And when oppressed with heat his sons pass by,
With hastening feet they'll seek its arches green,
And bless the Father who has o'er them spread
A tent of verdure for each aching head.

To Him that Hath shall be Given.

WHY readest thou? thou canst not gain the life
The spirit leads, but by the spirit's toil;
The labor of the body is not strife
Such as will give to thee the wine and oil;

To him who hath, to him my verse shall give,
And he the more from all he does shall gain;
The spirit's life he too shall learn to live,
And share on earth in hope the spirit's pain;
Be taught of God; none else can teach thee aught;
He will thy steps forever lead aright;
The life is all that He his sons has taught;
Obey within, and thou shalt see its light,
And gather from its beams a brighter ray,
To cheer thee on along thy doubtful way.

Who hath Ears to Hear, let him Hear.

THE sun doth not the hidden place reveal,
Whence pours at morn his golden flood of light;
But what the night's dark breast would fain con-
        ceal,
In its true colors stands before our sight;
The bird doth not betray the secret springs,
Whence note on note her music sweetly pours;
Yet turns the ear attentive while she sings,
The willing heart, while falls the strain, adores.
So shall the Spirit tell not whence its birth,
But in its light thine untold deeds lay bare;
And while it walks with thee, flesh-clothed, the
        earth,
Its words shall of the Father's love declare;
And happy those whose ears shall hail its voice,
And clean within the day it gives rejoice.

𝔗𝔥𝔢 𝔖𝔬𝔫.

FATHER, I wait thy word.   The sun doth stand
Beneath the mingling line of night and day,
A listening servant, waiting thy command
To roll rejoicing on its silent way;
The tongue of time abides the appointed hour,
Till on our ear its solemn warnings fall;
The heavy cloud withholds the pelting shower,
Then every drop speeds onward at thy call;
The bird reposes on the yielding bough,
With breast unswollen by the tide of song;
So does my spirit wait thy presence now
To pour thy praise in quickening life along,
Chiding with voice divine man's lengthened sleep,
While round the Unuttered Word and Love their
      vigils keep.

𝔍𝔫 𝔥𝔦𝔪 𝔴𝔢 𝔏𝔦𝔳𝔢.

FATHER! I bless thy name that I do live,
And in each motion am made rich with Thee,
That when a glance is all that I can give,
It is a kingdom's wealth, if I but see;
This stately body cannot move, save I
Will to its nobleness my little bring;
My voice its measured cadence will not try,

Save I with every note consent to sing;
I cannot raise my hands to hurt or bless,
But I with every action must conspire
To show me there how little I possess,
And yet that little more than I desire;
May each new act my new allegiance prove,
Till in thy perfect love I ever live and move.

Time.

THERE is no moment but whose flight doth bring
Bright clouds and fluttering leaves to deck my
　　　bower;
And I, within, like some sweet bird must sing
To tell the story of the passing hour;
For time has secrets that no bird has sung,
Nor changing leaf with changing season told;
They wait the utterance of some nobler tongue
Like that which spoke in prophet tones of old;
Then day and night, and month and year shall
　　　tell
The tale that speaks but faint from bird and
　　　bough;
In spirit-songs their praise shall upward swell,
Nor longer pass heaven's gate unheard as now,
But cause e'en angels' ears to catch the strain,
And send it back to earth in joy again.

The Star.

Thou mak'st me poor that I enriched by Thee
May tell thy love to those who know it not;
And rise within thy heavens a star to be,
When they, thine earthly suns, are all forgot;
Grant that my light may through their darkness
      shine
With increased splendor from the parent
      source,
A diamond fashioned by the hand divine
To hold forever on its measured course;
But I am dark as yet, but soon the light
Of thy bright morning star on me shall dawn, —
Sure herald that the curtain of the night
Forever from my orb shall be withdrawn,
And its pure beams thy rays shall ever boast,
Shining accepted 'mid the starry host.

The Idler.

I idle stand that I may find employ,
Such as my Master when He comes will give;
I cannot find in mine own work my joy,
But wait, although in waiting I must live;
My body shall not turn which way it will,
But stand till I the appointed road can find,

And journeying so his messages fulfill,
And do at every step the work designed.
Enough for me, still day by day to wait
Till Thou who form'st me find'st me too a task;
A cripple lying at the rich man's gate,
Content for the few crumbs I get to ask;
A laborer but in heart, while bound my hands
Hang idly down still waiting thy commands.

The Hand and Foot.

THE hand and foot that stir not, they shall find
Sooner than all the rightful place to go:
Now in their motion free as roving wind,
Though first no snail so limited and slow;
I mark them full of labor all the day,
Each active motion made in perfect rest;
They cannot from their path mistaken stray,
Though 't is not theirs, yet in it they are blest;
The bird has not their hidden track found out,
The cunning fox though full of art he be;
It is the way unseen, the certain route,
Where ever bound, yet thou art ever free;
The path of Him, whose perfect law of love
Bids spheres and atoms in just order move.

The Disciple.

Thou wilt my hands employ, though others find
No work for those who praise thy name aright;
And in their worldly wisdom call them blind,
Whom Thou hast blest with thine own Spirit's
       sight.
But while they find no work for Thee to do,
And blindly on themselves alone rely;
The child must suffer what Thou sufferest too,
And learn from him Thou send'st e'en so to die;
Thou art my Father, Thou wilt give me aid
To bear the wrong the spirit suffers here;
Thou hast thy help upon the mighty laid; —
In Thee I trust, nor know to want or fear,
But ever onward walk, secure from sin,
For Thou hast conquered every foe within.

The Clay.

Thou shalt do what Thou wilt with thine own
       hand,
Thou form'st the spirit like the moulded clay;
For those who love Thee keep thy just command,
And in thine image grow as they obey;
New tints and forms with every hour they take
Whose life is fashioned by thy Spirit's power;

The crimson dawn is round them when they
      wake,
And golden triumphs wait the evening hour;
The queenly-sceptred night their souls receives,
And spreads their pillows 'neath her sable tent;
Above them Sleep their palm with poppy weaves,
Sweet rest Thou hast to all who labor lent;
That they may rise refreshed to light again
And with Thee gather in the whitening grain.

The Earth.

I WOULD lie low — the ground on which men
      tread —
Swept by thy Spirit like the wind of heaven;
An earth, where gushing springs and corn for
      bread
By me at every season should be given;
Yet not the water or the bread that now
Supplies their tables with its daily food,
But they should gather fruit from every bough,
Such as Thou givest me, and call it good;
And water from the stream of life should flow,
By every dwelling that thy love has built,
Whose taste the ransomed of thy Son shall know,
Whose robes are washed from every stain of
      guilt;
And men would own it was thy hand that blest,
And from my bosom find a surer rest.

The River.

Oh ! swell my bosom deeper with thy love,
That I some river's widening mouth may be;
And ever on, for many a mile above,
May flow the floods that enter from thy sea;
And may they not retreat as tides of earth,
Save but to show from Thee that they have
   flown,
Soon may my spirit find that better birth,
Where the retiring wave is never known;
But Thou dost flow through every channel wide,
With all a Father's love in every soul;
A stream that knows no ebb, a swelling tide
That rolls forever on and finds no goal,
Till in the hearts of all shall opened be
The ocean depths of thine eternity.

The House.

I BUILD a house, but in this 't will appear
That I have built it not, a shining forth
Of that bright palace that from year to year
New pillars has and domes from mine own worth;
The wondrous hand that forms it, in the sea,
In crystal depths fashions the coral pile,
The sun-lit roof that o'er our heads we see,

Earth's grassy plain that stretches many a mile :
'T is round me like the morning's presence, felt
As that in which apart I live from all ;
A zone that girds me like Orion's belt,
That I be seen the more on that bright wall,
Where all as golden constellations shine
With their own light, yet lit with Light Divine.

Day unto Day uttereth Speech.

I WOULD adorn the day and give it voice,
That it should sing with praises meet for Thee;
For none but man can bid it so rejoice,
That it shall seem a joyful day to me;
Break forth ye hearts that frozen winters bind
In icy chains more strong than close the year!
Look up! the day, the day, ye suffering blind!
Ye deaf, its notes of welcome come and hear!
Bid it the joy your hearts have long supprest
Give back to you in new awakening strains;
To rouse the sinful from their guilty rest,
And break the captive's more than iron chains;
It shall arise with healing in its beams,
And wake the nations from their lengthened
    dreams.

The New Birth.

The New Birth.

'T is a new life; — thoughts move not as they
      did,
With slow uncertain steps across my mind;
In thronging haste fast pressing on they bid
The portals open to the viewless wind,
That comes not save when in the dust is laid
The crown of pride that gilds each mortal brow,
And from before man's vision melting fade
The heavens and earth; — their walls are falling
      now.
Fast crowding on, each thought asks utterance
      strong;
Storm-lifted waves swift rushing to the shore,
On from the sea they send their shouts along,
Back through the cave-worn rocks their thunders
      roar;
And I, a child of God by Christ made free,
Start from death's slumbers to eternity.

4

The New World.

THE night that has no star lit up by God,
The day that round men shines who still are
        blind,
The earth their grave-turned feet for ages trod,
And sea swept over by His mighty wind, —
All these have passed away; — the melting dream
That flitted o'er the sleeper's half-shut eye,
When touched by morning's golden-darting
        beam; —
And he beholds around the earth and sky
That ever real stands, the rolling shores
And heaving billows of the boundless main,
That show, though time is past, no trace of years.
And earth restored he sees as his again,
The earth that fades not and the heavens that
        stand,
Their strong foundations laid by God's right
        hand.

The Garden.

I SAW the spot where our first parents dwelt;
And yet it wore to me no face of change,
For while amid its fields and groves, I felt
As if I had not sinned, nor thought itstrange;

My eye seemed but a part of every sight,
My ear heard music in each sound that rose;
Each sense forever found a new delight,
Such as the spirit's vision only knows;
Each act some new and ever-varying joy
Did by my Father's love for me prepare;
To dress the spot my ever fresh employ,
And in the glorious whole with Him to share;
No more without the flaming gate to stray,
No more for sin's dark stain the debt of death to
    pay.

The Presence.

I SIT within my room, and joy to find
That Thou, who always lov'st, art with me here;
That I am never left by Thee behind,
But by thyself Thou keep'st me ever near.
The fire burns brighter when with Thee I look,
And seems a kinder servant sent to me;
With gladder heart I read thy holy book,
Because Thou art the eyes by which I see;
This aged chair, that table, watch, and door
Around in ready service ever wait;
Nor can I ask of Thee a menial more
To fill the measure of my large estate,
For Thou thyself, with all a Father's care,
Where'er I turn, art ever with me there.

The Spirit Land.

FATHER! thy wonders do not singly stand,
Nor far removed where feet have seldom strayed;
Around us ever lies the enchanted land,
In marvels rich to thine own sons displayed.
In finding Thee are all things round us found;
In losing Thee are all things lost beside:
Ears have we, but in vain strange voices sound,
And to our eyes the vision is denied;
We wander in a country far remote,
Mid tombs and ruined piles in death to dwell;
Or on the records of past greatness dote,
And for a buried soul the living sell;
While on our path bewildered falls the night
That ne'er returns us to the fields of light.

The Ark.

THERE is no change of time and place with
          Thee;
Where'er I go, with me 't is still the same;
Within thy presence I rejoice to be,
And always hallow thy most holy name.
The world doth ever change; there is no peace
Among the shallows of its storm-vexed breast;

With every breath the frothy waves increase,
They toss up mire and dirt, they cannot rest.
I thank Thee that within thy strong-built ark
My soul across the uncertain sea can sail,
And though the night of death be long and dark,
My hopes in Christ shall reach within the vail;
And to the promised haven steady steer,
Whose rest to those who love is ever near.

The Living God.

THERE is no death with Thee! each plant and
     tree
In living haste their stems push onward still,
The pointed blade, each rooted trunk we see,
In various movement all attest thy will.
The vine must die when its long race is run;
The tree must fall when it no more can rise, —
The worm has at its root his task begun,
And hour by hour his steady labor plies.
Nor man can pause, but in thy will must grow,
And, as his roots within more deep extend,
He shall o'er sons of sons his branches throw,
And to the latest born his shadows lend;
Nor know in Thee disease nor length of days,
But lift his head forever in thy praise.

Life.

It is not life upon Thy gifts to live,
But to grow fixed with deeper roots in Thee;
And when the sun and shower their bounties
          give,
To send out thick-leaved limbs, a fruitful tree,
Whose green head meets the eye for many a
          mile,
Whose moss-grown arms their rigid branches
          rear,
And full-faced fruits their blushing welcome smile,
As to its goodly shade our feet draw near;
Who tastes its gifts shall never hunger more,
For 't is the Father spreads the pure repast,
Who, while we eat, renews the ready store,
Which at his bounteous board must ever last;
For all the bridegroom's supper shall attend,
Who humbly hear and make his Word their
          friend.

Change.

Father! there is no change to live with Thee,
Save that in Christ I grow from day to day,
In each new word I hear, each thing I see,
I but rejoicing hasten on the way.

The morning comes with blushes overspread,
And I new-wakened find a morn within;
And in its modest dawn around me shed,
Thou hear'st the prayer and the ascending hymn.
Hour follows hour, the lengthening shades de-
       scend,
Yet they could never reach as far as me,
Did not thy love its kind protection lend,
That I a child might rest awhile on Thee,
Till to the light restored by gentle sleep,
With new-found zeal I might thy precepts keep.

Night.

I THANK thee, Father, that the night is near
When I this conscious being may resign,
Whose only task thy words of love to hear,
And in thy acts to find each act of mine;
A task too great to give a child like me,
The myriad-handed labors of the day,
Too many for my closing eyes to see,
Thy words too frequent for my tongue to say.
Yet when Thou see'st me burthened by thy love,
Each other gift more lovely then appears,
For dark-robed Night comes hovering from above,
And all thine other gifts to me endears;
And while within her darkened couch I sleep,
Thine eyes untired above will constant vigils
       keep.

Morning.

THE light will never open sightless eyes,
It comes to those who willingly would see;
And   every   object — hill,   and   stream,   and
        skies —
Rejoice within th' encircling line to be.
'T is day, — the field is filled with busy hands,
The shop resounds with noisy workmen's din,
The traveler with his staff already stands
His yet unmeasured journey to begin;
The light breaks gently, too, within the breast, —
Yet there no eye awaits the crimson morn,
The forge and noisy anvil are at rest,
Nor men nor oxen tread the fields of corn,
Nor pilgrim lifts his staff, — it is no day
To those who find on earth their place to stay.

The Journey.

To tell my journeys, where I daily walk,
These words thou hear'st me use were given me;
Give heed, then, when with thee my soul would
        talk,
That thou the path of peace it goes may see.
I know nowhere to turn, each step is new,
No wish before me flies to point the way;

But on I travel, with no end in view,
Save that from Him who leads I may not stray.
He knows it all; the turning of the road,
Where this way leads and that, He knows it
    well, •
And finds for me at night a safe abode,
Though I all houseless know not where to dwell.—
And can'st thou tell then where my journeying
    lies?
If so, thou tread'st with me the same blue skies.

Day.

DAY! I lament that none can hymn thy praise
In fitting strains, of all thy riches bless;
Though thousands sport them in thy golden rays,
Yet none like thee their Maker's name confess.
Great fellow of my being! woke with me
Thou dost put on thy dazzling robes of light,
And onward from the east go forth to free
Thy children from the bondage of the night.
I hail thee, pilgrim! on thy lonely way,
Whose looks on all alike benignant shine;
A child of light, like thee, I cannot stay,
But on the world I bless must soon decline,
New rising still, though setting to mankind,
And ever in the eternal West my dayspring find.

Humility.

Oh, humble me! I cannot bide the joy
That in my Saviour's presence ever flows;
May I be lowly, lest it may destroy
The peace his childlike spirit ever knows.
I would not speak thy word, but by Thee stand,
While Thou dost to thine erring children speak;
Oh, help me but to keep his own command,
And in my strength to feel me ever weak;
Then in thy presence shall I humbly stay,
Nor lose the life of love He came to give;
And find at last the life, the truth, the way
To where with Him thy blessed servants live;
And walk forever in the path of truth —
A servant yet a son; a sire and yet a youth.

The Message.

Yourself.

'T is to yourself I speak; you cannot know
Him whom I call in speaking such a one,
For you beneath the earth lie buried low,
Which he alone as living walks upon:
You may at times have heard him speak to you,
And often wished perchance that you were he;
And I must ever wish that it were true,
For then you could hold fellowship with me:
But now you hear us talk as strangers, met
Above the room wherein you lie abed;
A word perhaps loud spoken you may get,
Or hear our feet when heavily they tread;
But he who speaks, or him who 's spoken to,
Must both remain as strangers still to you.

The Eye and Ear.

Thou readest, but each lettered word can give
Thee but the sound that thou first gave to it;
Thou lookest on the page, things move and live,
In light thine eye, and thine alone, has lit;
Ears are there yet unstopped, and eyes unclosed,
That see and hear as in one common day,

When they which present see have long reposed,
And he who hears has mouldered, too, to clay :
These ever see and hear ; they are in Him
Who speaks, and all is light ; how dark before !
Each object throws aside its mantle dim,
Which hid the starry robe that once it wore,
And shines full born, disclosing all that is,
Itself by all things seen and owned as His.

The Lost.

THE fairest day that ever yet has shone,
Will be when thou the day within shalt see ;
The fairest rose that ever yet has blown,
When thou the flower thou lookest on shalt be.
But thou art far away among Time's toys ;
Thyself the day thou lookest for in them,
Thyself the flower that now thine eye enjoys,
But wilted now thou hang'st upon thy stem.
The bird thou hearest on the budding tree,
Thou hast made sing with thy forgotten voice ;
But when it swells again to melody,
The song is thine in which thou wilt rejoice ;
And thou new risen 'midst these wonders live,
That now to them dost all thy substance give.

The Narrow Way.

WHERE this one dwells and that, thou know'st
      it well,
Each earthly neighbor and each earthly friend;
But He who calls thee has no place to dwell,
And canst thou then thine all unto Him lend?
Canst thou a stranger be, where now well
      known;
Where now thou oftenest go'st, go nevermore,
But walk the world thenceforth thy way alone,
Broadening the path but little worn before?
Then may'st thou find me, when thou 't faint and
      weak,
And the strait road seems narrower still to grow;
For I will words of comfort to thee speak,
And onward with thee to my home I 'll go,
Where thou shalt find a rest in labor sweet,
No friend and yet a friend in all to greet.

The Created.

THERE is naught for thee by thy haste to gain;
'T is not the swift with Me that win the race;
Through long endurance of delaying pain,
Thine opened eye shall see thy Father's face;
Nor here nor there, where now thy feet would
      turn,

Thou wilt find Him who ever seeks for thee ;
But let obedience quench desires that burn,
And where thou art thy Father, too, will be.
Behold ! as day by day the spirit grows,
Thou see'st by inward light things hid before ;
Till what God is, thyself, his image, shows ;
And thou wilt wear the robe that first thou wore.
When bright with radiance from his forming
       hand,
He saw the lord of all his creatures stand.

The Apostles.

THE words that come unuttered by the breath,
Looks without eyes, these lighten all the globe ;
They are the ministering angels, sent where
       Death
Has walked the earth so long in seraph's robe ;
See crowding to their touch the groping blind !
And ears long shut to sound are bent to hear,
Quick as they speak the lame new vigor find,
And language to the dumb man's lips is near ;
Hail, sent to us, ye servants of high heaven !
Unseen, save by the humble and the poor ;
To them glad tidings have your voices given ;
For them their faith has wrought the wished-for
       cure ;
And ever shall they witness bear of you,
That He who sent you forth to heal was true.

The Slaveholder.

WHEN comes the sun to visit thee at morn,
Art thou prepared to give him welcome then;
Or is the day that with his light is born,
With thee a day that has already been;
Hast thou filled up its yet unnumbered hours
With thy heart's thoughts, and made them now
      thine own?
Then for thee cannot bloom its budding flowers;
The day to thee hast past, and onward flown;
The noon may follow with its quickening heat,
The grain grow yellow in its ripening rays,
And slow-paced evening mark the noon's retreat,
Yet thou as dead to them live all thy days;
For thou hast made of God's free gifts a gain,
And would'st the sovereign day a slave in bonds
      retain.

The Slave.

I SAW him forging link by link his chain,
Yet while he felt its length he thought him free,
And sighed for those borne o'er the barren main
To bondage that to his would freedom be;
Yet on he walked with eyes far-gazing still
On wrongs that from his own dark bosom flowed,

5

And while he thought to do his master's will
He but the more his disobedience showed.
I heard a wild rose by the stony wall,
Whose fragrance reached me in the passing gale,
A lesson give — it gave alike to all —
And I repeat the moral of its tale,
"That from the spot where deep its dark roots
     grew
Bloomed forth the fragrant rose that all delight
     to view."

The Morning Watch.

'T is near the morning watch : the dim lamp burns,
But scarcely shows how dark the slumbering
     street ;
No sound of life the silent mart returns ;
No friends from house to house their neighbors
     greet.
It is the sleep of death, — a deeper sleep
Than e'er before on mortal eyelids fell ;
No stars above the gloom their places keep ;
No faithful watchmen of the morning tell ;
Yet still they slumber on, though rising day
Hath through their windows poured the awaken-
     ing light ;
Or, turning in their sluggard trances, say, —
"There yet are many hours to fill the night."
They rise not yet ; while on the Bridegroom goes
Till He the day's bright gates forever on them
     close.

The Dead.

I SEE them, — crowd on crowd they walk the
    earth,
Dry leafless trees no autumn wind laid bare ;
And in their nakedness find cause for mirth,
And all unclad would winter's rudeness dare ;
No sap doth through their clattering branches
    flow,
Whence springing leaves and blossoms bright
    appear ;
Their hearts the living God have ceased to know
Who gives the spring-time to th' expectant year.
They mimic life, as if from Him to steal
His glow of health to paint the livid cheek ;
They borrow words for thoughts they cannot
    feel,
That with a seeming heart their tongue may
    speak ;
And in their show of life more dead they live
Than those that to the earth with many tears
    they give.

The Graveyard.

My heart grows sick before the wide-spread
    death
That walks and speaks in seeming life around ;

And I would love the corpse without a breath,
That sleeps forgotten 'neath the cold, cold
　　　ground;
For these do tell the story of decay,
The worm and rotten flesh hide not nor lie;
But this, though dying, too, from day to day,
With a false show doth cheat the longing eye,
And hide the worm that gnaws the core of life,
With painted cheek and smooth, deceitful skin;
Covering a grave with sights of darkness rife,
A secret cavern filled with death and sin;
And men walk o'er these graves and know it not,
For in the body's health the soul's forgot.

The Prison.

THE prison-house is full; there is no cell
. But hath its prisoner laden with his chains;
And yet they live as though their life was well,
Nor of its burdening sin the soul complains;
Thou dost not see where thou hast lived so
　　　long, —
The place is called the skull where thou dost
　　　tread.
Why laugh'st thou, then, why sing the sportive
　　　song,
As if thou livest, and know'st not thou art dead.
Yes, thou art dead, the morn breaks o'er thee
　　　now, —

Where is thy Father, He who gave thee birth?
Thou art a severed limb, a barren bough,
Thou sleepest in deep caverns of the earth.
Awake! thou hast a glorious race to run;
Put on thy strength, thou hast not yet begun.

He was acquainted with Grief.

I CANNOT tell the sorrows that I feel
By the night's darkness, by the prison's gloom;
There is no sight that can the death reveal
The spirit suffers in a living tomb;
There is no sound of grief that mourners raise,
No moaning of the wind, or dirge-like sea,
Nor hymns, though prophet tones inspire the lays,
That can the Spirit's grief awake in thee.
Thou, too, must suffer, as it suffers here,
The death in Christ to know the Father's love;
Then in the strains that angels love to hear
Thou, too, shalt hear the Spirit's song above,
And learn in grief what these can never tell, —
A note too deep for earthly voice to swell.

Faith.

THERE is no faith: the mountain stands within
Still unrebuked, its summit reaches heaven ;
And every action adds its load of sin,
For every action wants the little leaven.
There is no prayer : it is but empty sound,
That stirs with frequent breath the yielding air,
With every pulse they are more strongly bound,
Who make the blood of goats the voice of prayer ;
Oh, heal them, — heal them, Father, with thy
        word,
Their sins cry out to Thee from every side :
From son and sire, from slave and master heard,
Their voices fill the desert country wide ;
And bid Thee hasten to relieve and save,
By Him who rose triumphant o'er the grave.

Enoch.

I LOOKED to find a man who walked with God,
Like the translated patriarch of old ; —
Though gladdened millions on his footstool trod,
Yet none with Him did such sweet converse hold.
I heard the wind in low complaint go by
That none its melodies like him could hear ; —
Day unto day spoke wisdom from on high,

Yet none like David turned a willing ear :
God walked alone, unhonored, through the earth.
For Him no heart-built temple open stood ;
The soul, forgetful of her nobler birth,
Had hewn Him lofty shrines of stone and wood,
And left unfinished, and in ruins still,
The only temple He delights to fill.

Worship.

THERE is no worship now : the idol stands
Within the Spirit's holy resting-place !
Millions before it bend with upraised hands,
And with their gifts God's purer shrine disgrace.
The prophet walks unhonored 'mid the crowd
That to the idol's temple daily throng ;
His voice unheard above their voices loud,
His strength too feeble 'gainst the torrent strong ;
But there are bounds that ocean's rage can stay
When wave on wave leaps madly to the shore :
And soon the prophet's word shall men obey,
And hushed to peace the billows cease to roar;
For He who spake — and warring winds kept
    peace,
Commands again — and man's wild passions
    cease.

Thy Brother's Blood.

I HAVE no brother.   They who meet me now
Offer a hand with their own wills defiled,
And, while they wear a smooth, unwrinkled brow,
Know not that Truth can never be beguiled.
Go wash the hand that still betrays thy guilt; —
Before the Spirit's gaze what stain can hide?
Abel's red blood upon the earth is spilt,
And by thy tongue it cannot be denied.
I hear not with the ear, — the heart doth tell
Its secret deeds to me untold before ;
Go, all its hidden plunder quickly sell,
Then shalt thou cleanse thee from thy brother's
          gore,
Then will I take thy gift; — that bloody stain
Shall not be seen upon thy hand again.

The Jew.

THOU art more deadly than the Jew of old :
Thou hast his weapons hidden in thy speech ;
And though thy hand from me thou dost with-.
          hold,
They pierce where sword and spear could never
          reach.
Thou hast me fenced about with thorny talk,

To pierce my soul with anguish while I hear;
And while amid thy populous streets I walk,
I feel at every step the entering spear.
Go, cleanse thy lying mouth of all its guile
That from the will within thee ever flows;
Go, cleanse the temple thou dost now defile,
Then shall I cease to feel thy heavy blows;
And come and tread with me the path of peace,
And from thy brother's harm forever cease.

The Poor.

I WALK the streets, and though not meanly drest,
Yet none so poor as can with me compare;
For none, though weary, call me in to rest,
And though I hunger, none their substance
    share.
I ask not for my stay the broken reed,
That fails when most I want a friendly arm;
I cannot on the loaves and fishes feed
That want the blessing that they may not harm.
I only ask the living word to hear
From tongues that now but speak to utter death;
I thirst for one cool cup of water clear,
But drink the riled stream of lying breath;
And wander on, though in my Fatherland,
Yet hear no welcome voice and see no beckoning
    hand.

𝔜e gabe me no 𝔐eat.

My brother, I am hungry : give me food
Such as my Father gives me at his board ;
He has for many years been to thee good,
Thou canst a morsel, then, to me afford.
I do not ask of thee a grain of that
Thou offerest when I call on thee for bread ;
This is not of the wine nor olive fat,
But those who eat of this like thee are dead.
I ask the love the Father has for thee,
That thou should'st give it back to me again ;
This shall my soul from pangs of hunger free,
And on my parchëd spirit fall like rain ;
Then thou wilt prove a brother to my need,
For in the cross of Christ thou, too, canst bleed.

𝔅read.

Long do we live upon the husks of corn,
While 'neath untasted lie the kernels still ;
Heirs of the kingdom, but in Christ unborn,
Fain with swine's food would we our hunger fill.
We eat, but 't is not of the bread from heaven ;
We drink, but 't is not from the stream of life ;
Our swelling actions want the little leaven
To make them with the sighed-for blessing rife ;

We wait unhappy on a stranger's board,
While we the master's friend by right should
    live,
Enjoy with him the fruits our labors stored,
And to the poor with him the pittance give;
No more to want, the long expected heir
With Christ the Father's love forevermore to
    share.

The Heart.

THERE is a cup of sweet or bitter drink,
Whose waters ever o'er the brim must well,
Whence flow pure thoughts of love as angels
    think,
Or of its dæmon depths the tongue will tell.
That cup can ne'er be cleansed from outward
    stains
While from within the tide forever flows;
And soon it wearies out the fruitless pains
The treacherous hand on such a task bestows;
But ever bright its crystal sides appear,
While runs the current from its outlet pure;
And pilgrims hail its sparkling waters near,
And stoop to drink the healing fountain sure,
And bless the cup that cheers their fainting soul
While through this parching waste they seek
    their heavenly goal.

Jacob's Well.

THOU pray'st not, save when in thy soul thou
        pray'st,
Disrobing of thyself to feed the poor;
The words thy lips shall utter then, thou say'st,
They are as marble, and they shall endure.
Pray always, for on prayer the hungry feed;
Its sound is hidden music to the soul,
From low desires its rising strains shall lead,
And willing captives own thy just control.
Draw not too often on the gushing spring,
But rather let its own o'erflowings tell
Where the cool waters rise, and thither bring
Those who more gladly then will hail the well;
When, gushing from within, new streams like
        thine
Shall bid them ever drink and own its source
        divine.

The Prophet.

THE Prophet speaks, the world attentive stands!
The voice that stirs the people's countless host,
Issues again the Living God's commands;
And who before the King of kings can boast?
At his rebuke behold a thousand flee,

Their hearts the Lord hath smitten with his fear;
Bow to the Christ, ye nations! bow the knee!
Repent! the kingdom of the Son is near!
Deep on their souls the mighty accents fall,
Like lead that pierces through the walls of clay;
Pricked to the heart the guilty spirits call
To know of Him the new, the living way;
They bow; for He can loose, and He can bind;
And in his path the promised blessing find.

Christmas.

AWAKE, ye dead! The summons has gone forth
That bids ye leave the dark inclosing grave;
From east to west 't is heard, from south to
   north
The word goes forth imprisoned souls to save:
Though ye have on the garments of the dead,
And the fourth day have slept within the earth,
Come forth! you shall partake the living bread,
And be a witness of the Spirit's birth.
Awake, ye faithful! throw your grave-clothes by,
He whom ye seek is risen, bids ye rise;
The cross again on earth is lifted high;
Turn to its healing sight your closing eyes;
And you shall rise and gird your armor on,
And fight till you a crown in Christ have won.

The Mountain.

THOU shalt the mountain move; be strong in me,
And I will pluck it from its rocky base,
And cast it headlong in the rolling sea, —
And men shall seek but shall not find its place.
Be strong; thou shalt throw down the numerous
        host
That rises now against thee o'er the earth;
Against thy Father's arm they shall not boast,
In sorrow shall grow dark their day of mirth.
Lift up the banner, bid the trumpets sound;
Gather, ye nations, on the opposing hill!
I will your wisest councils now confound,
And all your ranks with death and slaughter fill.
I come for judgment, and for victory now,
Bow down, ye nations! at my footstool bow!

The Things Before.

I WOULD not tarry.   Look! the things before
Call me along my path with beckoning love;
The things I gain wear not the hues they wore,
For brighter glories gild the heavens above.
Still on, I seek the peace the Master sought,
The world cannot disturb his joy within;
It is not with its gold and silver bought,

It is the victory over death and sin.
But those who enter the bright city's gates,
Ride low on one the marked and scorned of
      earth ;
For there the ready mansion open waits
For those who live rejected from their birth;
And He who went before them bids, all hail !
To those who o'er the world in Him prevail.

The Soul's Rest.

REJOICE, ye weary ! ye whose spirits mourn,
There is a rest which shall not be removed ;
Press on and reach within the heavenly bourne,
By Christ, the King of your salvation proved.
There is a rest ! Rejoice, ye silent stars,
Roll on no more all voiceless on your way :
Thou Sun ! No more dark cloud thy triumph
      bars, —
Speak thou to every land the coming day.
And thou, my soul, that feel'st the rest within,
That greater art than star or burning sun,
Rejoice! for thou hast known the rest from sin,
And hast the eternal life in God begun ; —
Praise thou the Lord with every living thing,
And for his grace with saints and angels sing.

Praise.

Oh praise the Lord! Let every heart be glad!
The day has come when He will be our God;
No fears can come to make his children sad,
His joy is theirs who in his ways have trod.
Oh praise, ye hills! Praise Him, ye rivers
     wide!
Ye people own his love! revere his power!
He makes his peace in one full current glide,
It shall flow on unbroken from this hour.
Shout! shout, ye saints! the triumph day is
     near,
The King goes forth Himself his sons to save;
The habitations of the poor to rear,
And bid the palm and myrtle round them wave!
Open your gates, ye heaven-uplifted walls!
The King of kings for entrance at them calls.

Nature.

Nature.

NATURE! my love for thee is deeper far
Than strength of words, though spirit-born, can
        tell ;
For while I gaze they seem my soul to bar,
That in thy widening streams would onward
        swell,
Bearing thy mirrored beauty on its breast, —
Now, through thy lonely haunts unseen to glide,
A motion that scarce knows itself from rest,
With pictured flowers and branches on its tide ;
Then, by the noisy city's frowning wall,
Whose armëd heights within its waters gleam,
To rush with answering voice to ocean's call,
And mingle with the deep its swollen stream,
Whose boundless bosom's calm alone can hold
That heaven of glory in thy skies unrolled.

The Song.

WHEN I would sing of crooked streams and
        fields,
On, on from me they stretch too far and wide,
And at their look my song all powerless yields,
(83)

And down the river bears me with its tide.
Amid the fields I am a child again,
The spots that then I loved I love the more,
My fingers drop the strangely-scrawling pen,
And I remember nought but Nature's lore.
I plunge me in the river's cooling wave,
Or on the embroidered bank admiring lean,
Now some endangered insect life to save,
Now watch the pictured flowers and grasses
   green ;
Forever playing where a boy I played,
By hill and grove, by field and stream delayed.

To the Pure all Things are Pure.

THE flowers I pass have eyes that look at me,
The birds have ears that hear my spirit's voice,
And I am glad the leaping brook to see,
Because it does at my light step rejoice.
Come, brothers, all who tread the grassy hill,
Or wander thoughtless o'er the blooming fields,
Come learn the sweet obedience of the will ;
Thence every sight and sound new pleasure
   yields.
Nature shall seem another house of thine,
When He who formed thee, bids it live and play,
And in thy rambles e'en the creeping vine
Shall keep with thee a jocund holiday,
And every plant, and bird, and insect be
Thine own companions born for harmony.

Nature.

The bubbling brook doth leap when I come by,
Because my feet find measure with its call;
The birds know when the friend they love is
    nigh,
For I am known to them both great and small;
The flowers that on the lovely hill-side grow
Expect me there when Spring their bloom has
    given;
And many a tree and bush my wanderings know,
And e'en the clouds and silent stars of heaven:
For he who with his Maker walks aright
Shall be their lord, as Adam was before;
His ear shall catch each sound with new delight,
Each object wear the dress which then it wore;
And he, as when erect in soul he stood,
Hear from his Father's lips, that all is good.

The Robe.

Each naked branch, the yellow leaf or brown,
The rugged rock, and death-deformëd plain,
Lie white beneath the winter's feathery down,
Nor doth a spot unsightly now remain.
On sheltering roof, on man himself, it falls;
But him no robe, not spotless snow, makes clean;

Beneath, his corse-like spirit ever calls,
That on it too may fall the heavenly screen.
But all in vain : its guilt can never hide
From the quick Spirit's heart-deep searching eye;
There barren plains and caverns yawning wide
Lie ever naked to the passer-by ;
Nor can one thought deformed the presence
     shun,
But to the Spirit's gaze stands bright as in the
     sun.

The Leafless Tree.

I TOO will wait with thee returning Spring,
When thick the leaves shall cling on every
     bough,
And birds within their new-grown arbor sing,
Unmindful of the storms that tear me now ;
For I have stript me naked to the blast
That now in triumph through my branches rides :
But soon the winter's bondage shall be past
To him who in the Saviour's love abides ;
And as his Father to thy limbs returns,
Blossom and bloom to sprinkle o'er thy dress,
So shall Christ call from out their funeral urns,
Those who in patience still their souls possess;
And clothe in raiment never to wax old,
All whom his Father gave him for his fold.

The Winter Rain.

THE rain comes down, it comes without our call,
Each pattering drop knows well its destined
      place,
And soon the fields whereon the blessings fall
Shall change their frosty look for Spring's sweet
      face;
So fall the words thy Holy Spirit sends,
Upon the heart where Winter's robe is flung;
They shall go forth as certain of their ends,
As the wet drops from out thy vapors wrung:
Spring will not tarry, though more late its rose
Shall bud and bloom upon the sinful heart;
Yet when it buds, forever there it blows,
And hears no Winter bid its bloom depart;
It strengthens with his storms, and grows more
      bright
When o'er the earth is cast his mantle white.

The Spirit.

I WOULD not breathe, when blows thy mighty
      wind
O'er desolate hill and winter-blasted plain,
But stand, in waiting hope, if I may find
Each flower recalled to newer life again,

That now unsightly hides itself from Thee,
Amid the leaves or rustling grasses dry,
With ice-cased rock and snowy-mantled tree,
Ashamed lest Thou its nakedness should spy;
But Thou shalt breathe, and every rattling bough
Shall gather leaves; each rock with rivers flow;
And they that hide them from thy presence now,
In new-found robes along thy path shall glow,
And meadows at thy coming fall and rise,
Their green waves sprinkled with a thousand
      eyes.

The Desert.

OH, bid the desert blossom as the rose,
For there is not one flower that meets me now;
On all thy fields lie heaped the wintry snows,
And the rough ice encrusts the fruitful bough.
Oh, breathe upon thy ruined vineyard still;
Though like the dead it long unmoved has lain,
Thy breath can with the bloom of Eden fill,
The lifeless clods in verdure clothe again.
Awake, ye slothful! open wide the earth
To the new sun and Spirit's quickening rain;
They came to bid the furrows heave in birth,
And strew with roses thick the barren plain.
Awake! be early in your untilled field,
And it to you the crop of peace shall yield.

Labor and Rest.

THOU need'st not rest: the shining spheres are
      thine
That roll perpetual on their silent way,
And Thou dost breathe in me a voice divine,
That tells more sure of thine eternal sway;
Thine the first starting of the early leaf,
The gathering green, the changing autumn hue;
To Thee the world's long years are but as brief
As the fresh tints that Spring will soon renew.
Thou needest not man's little life of years,
Save that he gather wisdom from them all;
That in thy fear he lose all other fears,
And in thy calling heed no other call.
Then shall he be thy child to know thy care,
And in thy glorious Self the eternal Sabbath
      share.

The Tree.

I LOVE thee when thy swelling buds appear
And one by one their tender leaves unfold,
As if they knew that warmer suns were near,
Nor longer sought to hide from Winter's cold;
And when with darker growth thy leaves are
      seen

To veil from view the early robin's nest,
I love to lie beneath thy waving screen
With limbs by summer's heat and toil opprest;
And when the autumn winds have stript thee
      bare,
And round thee lies the smooth, untrodden snow,
When nought is thine that made thee once so
      fair,
I love to watch thy shadowy form below,
And through thy leafless arms to look above
On stars that brighter beam when most we need
      their love.

The April Snow.

It will not stay! the robe so pearly white,
Which fell in folds in Nature's bosom bare,
And sparkled in the winter moonbeams' light,
A vesture such as sainted spirits wear.
It will not stay. Look, from the open plain,
It melts beneath the glance of April's sun;
Nor can the rock's cool shade the snow detain,
It feeds the brooks, which down the hillside run.
Why should it linger? Many tinted flowers
And the green grass its place will quickly fill,
And, with new life from sun and kindly showers,
With beauty deck the meadow and the hill,
Till we regret to see the earth resume
This snowy mantle for her robe of bloom.

The True Light.

THE morning's brightness cannot make thee
    glad,
If thou art not more bright than it within;
And nought of evening's peace hast thou e'er
    had,
If evening first did not with thee begin.
Full many a sun I saw first set and rise,
Before my day had found a rising too;
And I with Nature learned to harmonize,
And to her times and seasons made me true.
How fair that new May morning when I rose
Companion of the sun for all the day;
O'er every hill and field where now he goes,
With him to pass, nor fear again to stray;
But 'neath the full-orbed moon's reflected light
Still onward keep my way till latest night.

The Wind-Flower.

THOU lookest up with meek, confiding eye,
Upon the clouded smile of April's face,
Unharmed, though Winter stands uncertain by
Eying with jealous glance each opening grace.
Thou trustest wisely! In thy faith arrayed,
More glorious thou than Israel's wisest King.

Such faith was His whom men to death betrayed,
As thine, who hear'st the timid voice of Spring,
While other flowers still hide them from her call
Along the river's brink and meadow bare.
Thee will I seek beside the stony wall,
And in thy trust with childlike heart would
  share,
O'erjoyed that in thy early leaves I find
A lesson taught by Him who loved all human
  kind.

The Violet.

Thou tellest truths unspoken yet by man,
By this thy lonely home and modest look ;
For he has not the eyes such truths to scan,
Nor learns to read from such a lowly book.
With him it is not life firm-fixed to grow
Beneath the outspreading oaks and rising pines,
Content this humble lot of thine to know,
The nearest neighbor of the creeping vines ;
Without fixed root he cannot trust, like thee,
The rain will know the appointed hour to fall,
But fears lest sun or shower may hurtful be,
And would delay or speed them with his call;
Nor trust like thee when wintry winds blow cold,
Whose shrinking form the withered leaves enfold,

The Columbine.

STILL, still my eye will gaze long fixed on thee,
Till I forget that I am called a man,
And at thy side fast-rooted seem to be,
And the breeze comes my cheek with thine to
     fan.
Upon this craggy hill our life shall pass, —
A life of summer days and summer joys, —
Nodding our honey-bells mid pliant grass
In which the bee, half-hid, his time employs;
And here we 'll drink with thirsty pores the rain,
And turn dew-sprinkled to the rising sun,
And look when in the flaming west again
His orb across the heaven its path has run;
Here left in darkness on the rocky steep,
My weary eyes shall close like folding flowers in
     sleep.

The Wild Rose of Plymouth.

UPON the Plymouth shore the wild rose blooms,
As when the Pilgrims lived beside the bay,
And scents the morning air with sweet perfumes;
Though new this hour, more ancient far than
     they;
More ancient than the wild, yet friendly race,

That roved the land before the Pilgrims came,
And here for ages found a dwelling-place,
Of whom our histories tell us but a name!
Though new this hour, out from the past it
        springs,
Telling this summer morning of earth's prime;
And happy visions of the future brings,
That reach beyond, e'en to the verge of time;
Wreathing earth's children in one flowery chain
Of love and beauty, ever to remain.

The Sabbatia.

THE sweet-briar rose has not a form more fair,
Nor are its hues more beauteous than thine own,
Sabbatia, flower most beautiful and rare!
In lonely spots blooming unseen, unknown.
So spiritual thy look, thy stem so light,
Thou seemest not from the dark earth to grow;
But to belong to heavenly regions bright,
Where night comes not, nor blasts of winter
        blow.
To me thou art a pure, ideal flower,
So delicate that mortal touch might mar;
Not born, like other flowers, of sun and shower,
But wandering from thy native home afar
To lead our thoughts to some serener clime,
Beyond the shadows and the storms of time.

The Robin.

Thou need'st not flutter from thy half-built nest,
Whene'er thou hear'st man's hurrying feet go by,
Fearing his eye for harm may on thee rest,
Or he thy young's unfinished cottage spy;
All will not heed thee on that swinging bough,
Nor care that round thy shelter spring the leaves,
Nor watch thee on the pool's wet margin now
For clay to plaster straws thy cunning weaves;
All will not hear thy sweet, outpouring joy,
That with morn's stillness blends the voice of
      song,
For over-anxious cares their souls employ,
That else upon thy music borne along
And the light wings of heart-ascending prayer
Had learned that Heaven is pleased thy simple
      joys to share.

To the Canary-Bird.

I cannot hear thy voice with others' ears,
Who make of thy lost liberty a gain;
And in thy tale of blighted hopes and fears
Feel not that every note is born with pain.
Alas! that with thy music's gentle swell
Past days of joy should through thy memory
      throng,

And each to thee their words of sorrow tell,
While ravished sense forgets thee in thy song.
The heart that on the past and future feeds,
And pours in human words its thoughts divine,
Though at each birth the spirit inly bleeds,
Its songs may charm the listening ear like thine;
And men with gilded cage and praise will try
To make the bard like thee forget his native sky.

The Stranger's Gift.

I FOUND, far culled from fragrant field and grove,
Each flower that makes our Spring a welcome
        guest;
In one sweet bond of brotherhood inwove
An osier band their leafy stalks compressed;
A stranger's hand had made their bloom my
        own,
And fresh their fragrance rested on the air;
His gift was mine — but he who gave unknown,
And my heart sorrowed though the flowers were
        fair.
Now oft I grieve to meet them on the lawn,
As sweetly scattered round my path they grow,
By One who on their petals paints the dawn,
And gilt with sunset splendors bids them glow,
For I ne'er asked "who steeps them in per-
        fume?"
Nor anxious sought His love who crowns them
        all with bloom.

The Rose.

THE rose thou show'st me has lost all its hue,
For thou dost seem to me than it less fair ;
For when I look I turn from it to you,
And feel the flower has been thine only care.
Thou could'st have grown as freely by its side
As spring these buds from out the parent stem,
But thou art from thy Father severed wide,
And turnest from thyself to look at them.
Thy words do not perfume the summer air,
Nor draw the eye and ear like this thy flower ;
No bees shall make thy lips their daily care,
And sip the sweets distilled from hour to hour ;
Nor shall new plants from out thy scattered seed,
O'er many a field the eye with beauty feed.

The Acorn.

THE seed has started, — who can stay it? See,
The leaves are sprouting high above the ground ;
Already o'er the flowers, its head ; the tree
That rose beside it and that on it frowned,
Behold! is but a small bush by its side.
Still on ! it cannot stop ; its branches spread ;
It looks o'er all the earth in giant pride :
The nations find upon its limbs their bread,

7

Its boughs their millions shelter from the heat,
Beneath its shade see kindreds, tongues, and all
That the wide world contains, they all retreat
Beneath the shelter of that acorn small
That late thou flung'st away; 't was the best gift
That Heaven e'er gave; — its head the low shall
      lift.

I was sick and in Prison.

THOU hast not left the rough-barked tree to grow
Without a mate upon the river's bank;
Nor dost Thou on one flower the rain bestow,
But many a cup the glittering drops has drank.
The bird must sing to one who sings again,
Else would her note less welcome be to hear;
Nor hast Thou bid thy word descend in vain,
But soon some answering voice shall reach my
      ear.
Then shall the brotherhood of peace begin,
And the new song be raised that never dies,
That shall the soul from death and darkness win,
And burst the prison where the captive lies;
And one by one, new-born, shall join the strain,
Till earth restores her sons to heaven again.

The Trees of Life.

FOR those who worship Thee there is no death,
For all they do is but with Thee to dwell:
Now while I take from Thee this passing breath,
It is but of thy glorious name to tell;
Nor words nor measured sounds have I to find,
But in them both my soul doth ever flow;
They come as viewless as the unseen wind,
And tell thy noiseless steps where'er I go;
The trees that grow along thy living stream,
And from its springs refreshment ever drink,
Forever glittering in thy morning beam
They bend them o'er the river's grassy brink,
And, as more high and wide their branches grow,
They look more fair within the depths below.

The Clouded Morning.

THE morning comes; and thickening fogs pre-
        vail,
Hanging like curtains all the horizon round,
And o'er the head in heavy stillness sail, —
So still is day it seems like night profound.
But see! the mists are stirring, rays of light
Pierce through the haze as struggling to be free;
The circle round grows every moment bright,

The sun is breaking forth; 't is he, 't is he!
Quick from before him flies each sluggish cloud,
His rays have touched the stream, have climbed
    the hill;
The sounds of life increase, all blending loud,
The hum of men, nor smallest thing is still;
But all have found a voice, and hail their king,
The words of man's high praise, and bird with
    fluttering wing.

The Fair Morning.

THE clear bright morning, with its scented air
And gayly waving flowers, is here again;
Man's heart is lifted with the voice of prayer,
And peace descends as falls the gentle rain.
The tuneful birds that all night long have slept,
Take up at dawn the evening's dying lay,
When sleep upon their eyelids gently crept,
And stole with stealthy craft their song away.
High overhead the forest's swaying boughs
Sprinkle with drops of dew the whistling boy,
As to the field he early drives his cows,
More than content with this his low employ.
And shall not joy uplift me when I lead
The flocks of Christ by the still streams to feed?

The Ramble.

THE plants that careless grow shall bloom and
    bud,
When wilted stands man's nicely tended flower;
E'en on the unsheltered waste, or pool's dark
    mud,
Spring bells and lilies fit for lady's bower.
Come with me, I will show you where they grow;
The tangled vines and boughs come push aside;
O'er yonder hill-top's craggy side we go,
Then by the path beyond we downward slide.
See, by yond pond where few but travelers pass,
Each lily opens wide its curious cup,
And here where now we track the unmown grass,
The wild-heath bell, surprised, is looking up
To view the strangers that thus far have sought
The flowers that in fair Nature's robe are
    wrought.

The Invitation.

STAY where thou art, thou need'st not further
    go,
The flower with me is pleading at thy feet;
The clouds, the silken clouds, above me flow,
And fresh the breezes come thy cheek to greet.

Why hasten on ; — hast thou a fairer home ?
Has God more richly blest the world than here,
That thou in haste would'st from thy country
    roam,
Favored by every month that fills the year ?
Sweet showers shall on thee here, as there, de-
    scend ;
The sun salute thy morn and gild thy eve:
Come, tarry here, for Nature is thy friend,
And we an arbor for ourselves will weave ;
And many a pilgrim, journeying on as thou,
Will grateful bless its shade, and list the wind-
    struck bough.

The Field and Wood.

WHENCE didst thou spring, or art thou yet un-
    born ;
Who treadst with slighting foot so swift along,
Where near thee rises green the bladed corn,
And from the tree pours forth the birds' new
    song ?
Thy heart is ever flutt'ring, ne'er at rest ;
A bird that e'er would soar with wily art,
Yet when she seems of what she wished possest,
She feels the strength from out her wings de-
    part.
Learn wisdom from the sweet, delaying voice,
And from its melody turn not thine ear ;

With springing grain in slow decay rejoice,
And thou at one shall be with all things here;
And thy desires, that now o'ertop the grain,
Shall with its growth a life like theirs sustain.

The Barberry-Bush.

THE bush that has most briars and bitter fruit, —
Wait till the frost has turned its green leaves
  red,
Its sweetened berries will thy palate suit,
And thou may'st find e'en there a homely bread.
Upon the hills of Salem, scattered wide,
Their yellow blossoms gain the eye in Spring;
And straggling e'en upon the turnpike's side,
Their ripened branches to your hand they bring.
I've plucked them oft in boyhood's early hour,
That then I gave such name and thought it true;
But now I know that other fruit as sour
Grows on what now thou callest *Me* and *You;*
Yet, wilt thou wait the Autumn that I see,
Will sweeter taste than these red berries be.

The Fruit.

THOU ripenest the fruits with warmer air
That Summer brings around thy goodly trees,
And Thou wilt grant a summer to my prayer,
And fruit shall glisten from these fluttering
      leaves ; .
A fruit that shall not with the winter fail,
He knows no winter who of it shall eat,
But on it lives, though outward storms assail,
Till it becomes in time his daily meat:
Then he shall in the fruit I give abound,
And hungry pilgrims hasten to the bough,
Where the true bread of life shall then be found,
Though nought they spy to give upon it now;
But pass it by, with sorrowing hearts that there
But leaves have grown where they the fruit
      would share.

The Harvest.

THEY love me not who at my table eat;
They live not on the bread that Thou hast given;.
The word Thou giv'st is not their daily meat,
The bread of life that cometh down from heaven.
They drink, but from their lips the waters dry,
There is no well that gushes up within;

And for the meat that perishes they cry,
When Thou has vexed their souls because of sin.
Oh, send thy laborers! Every hill and field
With the ungathered crop is whitened o'er;
To those who reap it shall rich harvests yield,
In full-eared grain all ripened for thy store; —
No danger can they fear who reap with Thee,
Though thick with storms the autumn sky may
    be.

The Latter Rain.

THE latter rain, — it falls in anxious haste
Upon the sun-dried fields and branches bare,
Loosening with searching drops the rigid waste,
As if it would each root's lost strength repair;
But not a blade grows green as in the spring,
No swelling twig puts forth its thickening leaves;
The robins only mid the harvests sing,
Pecking the grain that scatters from the sheaves:
The rain falls still, — the fruit all ripened drops,
It pierces chestnut burr and walnut shell,
The furrowed fields disclose the yellow crops,
Each bursting pod of talents used can tell,
And all that once received the early rain
Declare to man it was not sent in vain.

The Frost.

THE frost is out, and in the open fields,
And late within the woods, I marked his track;
The unwary flower his icy fingers feels,
And at their touch the crispëd leaf rolls back; —
Look, how the maple o'er a sea of green
Waves in the autumnal wind his flag of red!
First struck of all the forest's spreading screen,
Most beauteous, too, the earliest of her dead.
Go on: thy task is kindly meant by Him
Whose is each flower and richly covered bough;
And though the leaves hang dead on every limb,
Still will I praise his love, that early now
Has sent before this herald of decay
        To bid me heed the approach of Winter's sterner
            day.

Autumn Days.

THE winds are out with loud increasing shout,
Where late before them walked the biting frost,
Whirling the leaves in their wild sport about,
And twig and limb athwart our path are tost.
But still the sun looks kindly on the year,
And days of summer warmth will linger yet;
And still the birds amid the fields we hear,

For the ripe grain and scattered seeds they get.
The shortening days grow slowly less and less,
And Winter comes with many a warning on ;
And still some day with kindly smile will bless,
Till the last hope's deceit is fledged and gone,
Before the deepening snows block up the way,
And the sweet fields are made of howling blasts
    the prey.

Autumn Leaves.

THE leaves, though thick, are falling : one by one
Decayed they drop from off their parent tree ;
Their work with Autumn's latest day is done, —
Thou see'st them borne upon the breezes free.
They lie strewn here and there, their many dyes
That yesterday so caught thy passing eye ;
Soiled by the rain each leaf neglected lies,
Upon the path where now thou hurriest by.
Yet think thee not their beauteous tints less fair
Than when they hung so gayly o'er thy head ;
But rather find thee eyes, and look thee there
Where now thy feet so heedless o'er them tread,
And thou shalt see, where wasting now they lie,
The unseen hues of immortality.

Song and Praise.

The Prayer.

WILT Thou not visit me?
The plant beside me feels thy gentle dew,
   And every blade of grass I see
From thy deep earth its quickening moisture
      drew.

Wilt Thou not visit me?
Thy morning calls on me with cheering tone;
   And every hill and tree
Lend but one voice, — the voice of Thee alone.

Come, for I need thy love,
More than the flower the dew or grass the rain;
   Come, gently as thy holy dove;
And let me in thy sight rejoice to live again.

I will not hide from them
When thy storms come, though fierce may be
      their wrath,
   But bow with leafy stem,
And strengthened follow on thy chosen path.

Yes, Thou wilt visit me:
Nor plant nor tree thine eye delights so well,
   As, when from sin set free,
My spirit loves with thine in peace to dwell.

The Coming of the Lord.

"Take ye heed, watch and pray : for ye know not when the time · is." — MARK xiii. 33.

COME suddenly, O Lord, or slowly come :
I wait thy will ; thy servant ready is :
Thou hast prepared thy follower a home, —
The heaven in which Thou dwellest, too, is his.

Come in the morn, at noon, or midnight deep ;
Come, for thy servant still doth watch and pray :
E'en when the world around is sunk in sleep,
I wake and long to see thy glorious day.

I would not fix the time, the day, nor hour,
When Thou with all thine angels shalt appear ;
When in thy kingdom Thou shalt come with
          power, —
E'en now, perhaps, the promised day is near !

For though in slumber deep the world may lie,
And e'en thy Church forget thy great command ;
Still, year by year, thy coming draweth nigh,
And in its power thy kingdom is at hand.

Not in some future world alone 't will be,
Beyond the grave, beyond the bounds of time ;
But on the earth thy glory we shall see,
And share thy triumph, peaceful, pure, sublime.

Lord, help me that I faint not, weary grow,
Nor at thy coming slumber, too, and sleep;
For Thou hast promised, and full well I know
Thou wilt to us thy word of promise keep.

The Call.

WHY art thou not awake, my son?
The morning breaks I formed for thee;
And I thus early by thee stand,
Thy new-awakening life to see.

Why art thou not awake, my son?
The birds upon the bough rejoice;
And I thus early by thee stand,
To hear with theirs thy tuneful voice.

Why sleep'st thou still? The laborers all
Are in my vineyard: hear them toil, —
As for the poor, with harvest song
They treasure up the wine and oil.
8

The Cottage.

THE house my earthly parent left
My heavenly parent still throws down,
For 't is of air and sun bereft,
Nor stars its roof with beauty crown.

He gave it me, yet gave it not
As one whose gifts are wise and good;
'T was but a poor and clay-built cot,
And for a time the storms withstood.

But lengthening years and frequent rain
O'ercame its strength : it tottered, fell,
And left me homeless here again, —
And where to go I could not tell.

But soon the light and open air
Received me as a wandering child,
And I soon thought their house more fair,
And all my grief their love beguiled.

Mine was the grove, the pleasant field
Where dwelt the flowers I daily trod;
And there beside them, too, I kneeled
And called their friend, my Father, God.

The Tenant.

TREES shall rise around thy dwelling,
When thy house from heaven appears.
Art thou that thou liv'st in selling,
As are numbered up thy years?

Thou canst ne'er have leave to enter
That new dwelling's open door;
Where thy hopes and wishes centre,
Where thy friend has gone before;

Till the hut where now thou livest
Low is leveled with the ground;
Then thy prayer to Him who givest
Has at length acceptance found.

Then, though poor, yet He will cherish,
Whose high mansion is the sky;
Houseless left, thou shalt not perish
'Neath its wide-spread canopy.

Quick, then, leave some poorer dweller
That wherein thou livest now;
Better far awaits the seller,
Richer lands his oxen plough.

Faith and Sight.

THE comings on of Faith,
The goings out of Sight,
Are as the brightening of the morn
And dying of the night.

Man tells not of the hour, —
By Him alone 't is told,
Who day and night with certain bounds
Marked out for him of old.

The singing of the bird,
And sinking of her strain;
The roar of ocean's storm-lashed waves
And lull the date retain.

The fading of the leaf,
And blending of each hue;
The coming hour still hold in truth,
When change the old and new.

There's nought in Nature's hymn,
Of earth, or sea, or sky,
But is prophetic of the time
When birth to death is nigh.

The Silent.

THERE is a sighing in the wood,
A murmur in the beating wave,
The heart has never understood
To tell in words the thoughts they gave.

Yet oft it feels an answering tone,
When wandering on the lonely shore ;
And could the lips its voice make known,
'T would sound as does the ocean's roar.

And oft beneath the wind-swept pine,
Some chord is struck the strain to swell;
Nor sounds nor language can define, —
'T is not for words or sounds to tell.

'T is all unheard, that Silent Voice,
Whose goings forth, unknown to all,
Bids bending reed and bird rejoice,
And fills with music Nature's hall.

And in the speechless human heart
It speaks, where'er man's feet have trod ;
Beyond the lips' deceitful art,
To tell of Him, the Unseen God.

The Immortal.

'T is not that Thou hast given to me
A form which mortals cannot see,
  That I rejoice ;
But that I know Thou art around,
And though there comes to me no sound,
  I hear thy voice.

'T is not that Thou hast given me place
Among a new and happy race,
  I serve thee, Lord ;
But that thy mercies never fail,
And shall o'er all my sins prevail,
  Through thine own word.

Its praise has gone abroad ; who hears,
He casts aside all earthly fears,
  By it he lives ;
It bids him triumph o'er the grave,
And him o'er death dominion gave, —
  Thy joy and peace it gives.

Hear it, ye poor ! and ye who weep !
Arise, who lie in sin's long sleep !
  'T is strong to free ;
Give ear and it shall lead you on,
Till you the crown again have won,
  And me and mine can see.

The Gifts of God.

The light that fills thy house at morn,
Thou canst not for thyself retain;
But all who with thee here are born,
It bids to share an equal gain.

The wind that blows thy ship along,
Her swelling sails cannot confine;
Alike to all the gales belong,
Nor canst thou claim a breath as thine.

The earth, the green out-spreading earth,
Why hast thou fenced it off from me?
Hadst thou than I a nobler birth,
Who callest thine a gift so free.

The wave, the blue encircling wave,
No chains can bind, no fetters hold!
Its thunders tell of Him who gave
What none can ever buy for gold.

The Sight of the Ocean.

I GAZED afar from the rocky hill,
As if I never could drink my fill
Of the prospect fair, the ocean wide,
The blue bright ocean on every side.

For with the prospect grew my mind,
And seemed in the vast expanse to find
A space for its flight, without shore or bound,
Save the sky above and the shore around.

But soon o'er my spirit a feeling stole, —
A sad, lonely feeling I could not control,
Which the sight of the ocean doth ever bring,
As if, like the soul, 't were a living thing.

The plaintive wave, as it broke on the shore,
Seemed sighing for rest for evermore,
And glad at length the land to reach,
And tell its tale to the silent beach.

So seemed it then to my wandering thought,
That in the vast prospect a home had sought;
The ship o'er the waters a port may find,
But never the longing and restless mind.

As night o'er the ocean its shadow threw,
And homeward the weary sea-bird flew,

I turned from the dark and rocky height,
With grateful heart to my hearth-stone bright.

The Morn.

WHENCE came this morn, this glorious morn,
That hill and valley love so well?
From Thee who gave me voice to sing,
For they, too, of thy bounty tell.

Look! how each leaf and grassy blade
Return the glances of the morn;
There is no beauty in the stream
But of its beauty, too, is born.

But none can tell how fair they are,
Who do not with the morning live;
And in its light find life with them,
And like them always praises give.

This morn, this brightly-beaming morn,
Then shall they know it came from Thee;
For they shall in its light rejoice,
And own that they thy children be.

The Shepherd's Life.

My flocks, had'st thou e'er seen them, where they
    feed
Upon the hills and flowery vestured plains,
And heard me pipe to them on shepherd's reed, —
Then would'st thou leave fore'er thy sordid gains,

And haste thee where the streams so gently flow,
Where sounding pines and rocks above me rise,
And seek this quiet life of mine to know,
And learn with me its simple joys to prize.

How quietly the morning melts away
Into the noon, while on the grass I lie;
And noon fades quickly into evening gray,
When troop the stars across the o'erhanging
    sky.

Here day by day I know nor want nor care,
For all I need has Love Paternal given;
And bid me, bounteous, all its blessings share,
And know on earth the bliss of those in heaven.

Thine be the shepherd's life, his cot be thine,
And may'st thou sit beside him at his board;
Then wilt thou cease to sorrow or repine,
And to the peace Christ gave him be restored.

Nature.

I LOVE to sit on the green hill's side,
That looks around on a prospect wide,
And send my mind far away to rove
O'er flowery meadow, and bending grove
That looks in the silent depths below
At the stranger woods that downward grow;
And fly o'er the face of the winding stream
With the beach bird that starts with a sudden
      scream;
Or skim with the gull the still, calm sea,
Where the white sail sleeps so peacefully;
Till I all forget in that waking dream,
But the sky, grove, sea, and winding stream.

And I hie me to the wood's green breast,
On the bird's light wing that seeks her nest,
With a swifter flight than she sprang away
To meet the bright steps of new-born day.
Hark! from the spot to mother so dear,
Break sweet the cries of young on mine ear.
See! on the sable pine grove afar
Rains silver light from Dian's bright car;
And stars steal downward with lovely ray,
As if from earth to call me away
To groves where the flowers of a deathless bloom
Breathe o'er a land unsullied by a tomb.

Oh, grant me an hour, an hour like this,
To drink from far purer streams of bliss
Than flow near the dusty paths of life,
Uptost by mad'ning passion and strife;
For my mind comes back with a lighter spring
Than the bird from her weary wandering, —
With a calm more deep than the still, bright sea,
Where the white sail sleeps so peacefully, —
To join the world of care again,
And look on the struggles and strife of men
With an eye that beams with as pure a ray
As called my soul from these scenes away.

The Swift.

MEN tell how many blossoms will appear
On every tree they plant and hope to thrive;
How many kernels fill the yellow ear,
How many bees shall swarm in every hive.

When Springs but come, 't is Autumn here with
      them;
And Summer but of Winter's cold can tell;
And when they see the fruit on laden stem,
With them its early buds begin to swell.

'T is all too slow, fair Nature's gentle growth,
Their hopes are ripe when hers but bud and
      bloom,

And they accuse her equal pace of sloth,
And cast on her the shadow of their gloom.

But she, kind mother of her children all,
With voice of dove-like meekness gently chides:
"I care for e'en the humble sparrow's fall,
Alike with yon bright orb that o'er thee glides."

The Hour.

I ASK not what the bud may be
That hangs upon the green-sheathed stem;
But love with every leaf I see,
To lie unfolded there like them.

I ask not what the tree may bear
When whitened by the hand of Spring;
But with its blossoms on the air,
Would far around my perfume fling.

The infant's joy is mine, — is mine;
I join its infant sports in glee,
And would not for a world resign
The look of love it casts on me.

Leave not the bird upon the wing,
But with her seek her shaded nest,
And then with voice like hers thou 'lt sing,
When life's last sunbeam gilds the west.

To-day.

I LIVE but in the present, — where art thou?
Hast thou a home in some past, future year?
I call to thee from every leafy bough,
But thou art far away and canst not hear.

Each flower lifts up its red or yellow head,
And nods to thee as thou art passing by:
Hurry not on, but stay thine anxious tread,
And thou shalt live with me, for there am I.

The stream that murmurs by thee heeds its voice,
Nor stop thine ear, 't is I that bid it flow;
And thou with its glad waters shalt rejoice,
And of the life I live within them know.

And hill, and grove, and flowers, and running
        stream,
When thou dost live with them shall look more
        fair;
And thou awake as from a cheating dream,
The life to-day with me and mine to share.

The Voice of God.

THEY told me, when my heart was glad,
And all around but said, rejoice, —
They told me, and it made me sad,
The thunder was God's angry voice.

And then I thought that from the sky,
Throned monarch o'er a guilty world,
His glance — the lightning flashing by —
His hand the bolts of ruin hurled.

But now I learn a holier creed
Than that my infancy was taught:
'T is from the words of love I read
That the sweet lips of Nature caught.

Yes, 't was my Father's voice I feared:
It fills the heaven, the wide-spread earth;
It called in every tone that cheered
Those rosy hours of childhood's mirth.

'T is only on the heedless ear
It breaks in thunder's pealing wrath,
Winging the wanderer's feet with fear
To fly destruction's flaming path.

God dwells no more afar from me,
In all that lives his voice is heard;

From the loud shout of rolling sea
To warbled song of morning's bird.

In all that stirs the human breast,
That wakes to mirth or draws the tear,
In passion's storm or soul's calm rest,
Alike the voice of God I hear

To the Painted Columbine.

BRIGHT image of the early years,
When glowed my cheek as red as thou,
And life's dark throng of cares and fears
Were swift-winged shadows o'er my sunny brow!

Thou blushest from the painter's page,
Robed in the mimic tints of art;
But Nature's hand in youth's green age
With fairer hues first traced thee on my heart.

The morning's blush, she made it thine,
The morn's sweet breath, she gave it thee,
And in thy look, my Columbine,
Each fond-remembered spot she bade me see.

I see the hill's far-gazing head,
Where gay thou noddest in the gale;
I hear light-bounding footsteps tread
The grassy path that winds along the vale.

I hear the voice of woodland song
Break from each bush and well-known tree,
And on light pinions borne along,
Comes back the laugh from childhood's heart of
    glee.

O'er the dark rock the dashing brook,
With look of anger, leaps again,
And, hastening to each flowery nook,
Its distant voice is heard far down the glen.

Fair child of art! thy charms decay,
Touched by the withered hand of Time;
And hushed the music of that day,
When my voice mingled with the streamlet's
    chime;

But on my heart thy cheek of bloom
Shall live when Nature's smile has fled;
And, rich with memory's sweet perfume,
Shall o'er her grave thy tribute incense shed.

There shalt thou live and wake the glee
That echoed on thy native hill;
And when, loved flower, I think of thee,
My infant feet will seem to seek thee still.

9

Autumn Flowers.

STILL blooming on, when Summer flowers all
    fade,
The golden-rods and asters fill the glade;
The tokens they of an Exhaustless Love
That ever to the end doth constant prove.

To one fair tribe another still succeeds,
As still the heart new forms of beauty needs;
Till these bright children of the waning year,
Its latest born, have come our souls to cheer.

They glance upon us from their fringëd eyes,
And to their look our own in love replies;
Within our hearts we find for them a place,
As for the flowers which early spring-time grace.

Despond not, traveler! On life's lengthened way,
When all thy early friends have passed away;
Say not, "No more the beautiful doth live,
And to the earth a bloom and fragrance give."

To every season has our Father given
Some tokens of his love to us from heaven;
Nor leaves us here, uncheered, to walk alone,
When all we loved and prized in youth have
    gone.

Let but thy heart go forth to all around,
Still by thy side the beautiful is found;
Along thy path the autumn flowers shall smile,
And to its close life's pilgrimage beguile.

To the Fossil Flower.

DARK fossil flower! I see thy leaves unrolled,
With all thy lines of beauty freshly marked,
As when the eye of Morn beamed on thee first,
And thou first turn'dst to meet its welcome smile.
And sometimes in the coals' bright rainbow
        hues
I dream I see the colors of thy prime,
And for a moment robe thy form again
In splendor not its own.   Flower of the past!
Now, as I look on thee, life's echoing tread
Falls noiseless on my ear, — the present dies;
And o'er my soul the thoughts of distant time,
In silent waves, like billows from the sea,
Come rolling on and on, with ceaseless flow,
Innumerable.   Thou may'st have sprung un-
        sown
Into thy noon of life, when first earth heard
Its Maker's sovereign voice; and laughing flowers
Waved o'er the meadows, hung on mountain
        crags,
And nodded in the breeze on every hill.
Thou may'st have bloomed unseen, save by the
        stars

That sang together o'er thy rosy birth,
And came at eve to watch thy folded rest.
None may have sought .thee on thy fragrant
     home,
Save light-voiced winds that round thy dwelling
     played,
Or seemed to sigh, as oft their wingëd haste
Compelled their feet to roam.   Thou may'st have
     lived
Beneath the light of later days, when man,
With feet free-roving as the homeless wind,
Scaled the thick-mantled height, coursed plains
     unshorn,
Breaking the solitude of nature's haunt
With voice that seemed to blend, in one sweet
     strain,
The mingled music of the elements.
And when against his infant frame they rose,
Uncurbed, unawed by his yet feeble hand,
And when the muttering storm, and shouting
     wave,
And rattling thunder, mated, round him raged,
And seemed at times like demon foes to gird,
Thou may'st have won with gentle look his
     heart,
And stirred the first warm prayer of gratitude,
And been his first, his simplest altar-gift.
For thee, dark flower, the kindling sun can
     bring
No more the colors that it gave, nor morn,

With kindly kiss, restore thy breathing sweets:
Yet may the mind's mysterious touch recall
The bloom and fragrance of thy early prime:
For He who to the lowly lily gave
A glory richer than to proudest king,
He painted not those darkly-shining leaves,
With blushes like the dawn, in vain; nor gave
To thee its sweetly-scented breath, to waste
Upon the barren air.   E'en though thou stood
Alone in nature's forest-home untrod,
The first-love of the stars and sighing winds,
The mineral holds with faithful trust thy form,
To wake in human hearts sweet thoughts of love,
Now the dark past hangs round thy memory.

The Old Road.

THE road is left that once was trod
By man and heavy-laden beast;
And new ways opened, iron-shod,
That bind the land from west to east.

I asked of Him, who all things knows,
Why none who lived now passed that way;
Where rose the dust the grass now grows?
A still, low voice was heard to say:

"Thou know'st not why I change the course
Of him who travels, learn to go; —

Obey the Spirit's gentle force,
Nor ask thee where the stream may flow.

" Man shall not walk in his own ways,
For he is blind and cannot see;
But let him trust, and lengthened days
Shall lead his feet to heaven and Me.

" Then shall the grass the path grow o'er,
That his own wilfulness has trod;
And man nor beast shall pass it more,
But he shall walk with Me, his God."

The Worm.

I saw a worm, — with many a fold
He spun himself a silken tomb;
And there in winter-time enrolled,
He heeded not the cold nor gloom.

Within a small snug nook he lay,
Nor snow nor sleet could reach him there,
Nor wind was felt in gusty day,
Nor biting cold of frosty air.

Spring comes with bursting buds and grass,
Around him stirs a warmer breeze;
The chirping insects by him pass, —
His hiding-place not yet he leaves.

But Summer came, its fervid breath
Was felt within the sleeper's cell ;
And waking from his sleep of death,
I saw him crawl from out his shell.

Slow and with pain he first moved on,
And of the dust he seemed to be ;
A day passed by, the worm was gone, —
He soared on golden pinions free.

The Winter Bird.

THOU sing'st alone on the bare wintry bough,
As if Spring with its leaves were around thee
    now ;
And its voice that was heard in the laughing
    rill,
And the breeze as it whispered o'er meadow and
    hill,
Still fell on thine ear, as it murmured along
To join the sweet tide of thine own gushing
    song.
Sing on — though its sweetness was lost on the
    blast,
And the storm has not heeded thy song as it
    passed,
Yet its music awoke in a heart that was near,
A thought whose remembrance will ever prove
    dear ;

Though the brook may be frozen, though silent
    its voice,
And the gales through the meadows no longer
    rejoice,
Still I felt, as my ear caught thy glad note of
    glee,
That my heart in life's winter might carol like
    thee.

To the Humming-Bird.

I CANNOT heal thy green gold breast,
Where deep those cruel teeth have prest,
Nor bid thee raise thy ruffled crest
    And seek thy mate,
Who sits alone within thy nest,
    Nor sees thy fate.

No more with him in summer hours
Thou 'lt hum amid the leafy bowers,
Nor hover round the dewy flowers,
    To feed thy young;
Nor seek, when evening darkly lowers,
    Thy nest high hung.

No more thou 'lt know a mother's care
Thy honeyed spoils at eve to share,
Nor teach thy tender brood to dare,
    With upward spring,

Their path through fields of sunny air,
    On new-fledged wing.

For thy return in vain shall wait
Thy tender young, thy fond, fond mate,
Till night's last stars beam forth full late
    On their sad eyes :
Unknown, alas, thy cruel fate,
    Unheard thy cries !

Lines

TO A WITHERED LEAF SEEN ON A POET'S TABLE.

POET's hand has placed thee there,
Autumn's brown and withered scroll !
Though to outward eye not fair,
Thou hast beauty for the soul,

Though no human pen has traced
On that leaf its learned lore,
Love Divine the page has graced, —
What can words discover more ?

Not alone dim Autumn's blast
Echoes from yon tablet sear, —
Distant music of the Past
Steals upon the poet's ear.

Voices sweet of summer hours,
Spring's soft whispers murmur by ;
Feathered songs from leafy bowers
Draw his listening soul on high.

Lines

TO ——— ON THE DEATH OF HIS FRIEND.

"Then shall the dust return to earth as it was, and the spirit
unto God who gave it."

SHE sleeps not where the gladsome earth
Its dark green growth of verdure waves,
And where the winds' low-whispering mirth
Steals o'er the silent graves.

She sleeps not where the wild rose lends
Its fragrance to the morning air,
And where thy form at evening bends
To raise the voice of prayer.

She sleeps not where the wandering wing
Of weary bird will oft repose,
And bid Death's lonely dwelling ring
When shades around it close.

She sleeps not there — the wild-flowers' blush
Would kindle up her closëd eye ;
She could not hear sweet music's gush
Pass all unheeded by.

Vain, vain would earth call forth again
Her children from their narrow bed;
The soul that loved her joyous strain
Has fled — forever fled.

The spirit's robe earth gave is there,
Where leans yon wild-flower's cheek of bloom,
Where rises oft thy voice of prayer, —
The spirit has no tomb.

Dedication.[1]

THE weight of years is on the pile
Our fathers raised to Thee, O God:
On this, our temple, rest thy smile,
Till bent with days its tower shall nod.

Thy word awoke, O Power Divine!
The hymn of praise in Nature's hall:
'T is man's high gift to rear thy shrine,
And on Thee as his Father call.

To pour in music's solemn strain ·
The heart's deep tide of grateful love;
And kindle in thine earthly fane
A spirit for his home above.

Thou bad'st him on thine altar lay
The holy thought, the pure desire;

[1] For the Dedication of the Church of the North Society in Salem, June 22, 1836.

That light within, a brighter ray
Than sunbeam's glance, or vestal fire.

'T will burn when Heaven's high altar flame
On yon blue height has ceased to glow;
And o'er earth's dark, dissolving frame
The sunlight of the Spirit throw.

Father! within thy courts we bow,
To ask thy blessing, seek thy grace:
Oh, smile upon thy children now!
Look down on this, thy hallowed place!

And when its trembling walls shall feel
Time's heavy hand upon them rest,
Thy nearer presence, Lord, reveal,
And make thy children wholly blest.

Memory.

Soon the waves so lightly bounding
   All forget the tempest blast;
Soon the pines so sadly sounding
   Cease to mourn the storm that's past.

Soon is hushed the voice of gladness
   Heard within the green wood's breast;
Yet come back no notes of sadness,
   No remembrance breaks its rest.

But the heart, — how fond 't will treasure
    Every note of grief and joy!
Oft come back the notes of pleasure,
    Grief's sad echoes oft annoy.

There still dwell the looks that vanish
    Swift as brightness of a dream;
Time in vain earth's smiles may banish,
    There undying still they beam.

The Bunch of Flowers.

I SAW a bunch of flowers, and Time
With withered hand was plucking one;
I wondering asked him, as I passed,
For what the thing I saw was done.

"My gifts are these, the flowers you see,
For her who comes I hold this rose;"
I looked: the nurse held out her child,
Just wakened from its sweet repose.

Its small hand clasped the prize with joy,
Each seemed the other to the eye;
But soon the flowers' bright leaves were strown,
And while I gazed a youth passed by.

The flower Time gave to him he held,
And more admired; and kept awhile;

Yet as I watched him on his way,
'T was dropped ere he had paced a mile.

Man kept it longer : 't was to him a gift,
And with it long was loath to part;
But as he journeyed on, I saw
The rose lay withered on his heart.

One aged came : still he received Time's gift;
But as he took it heaved a sigh :
It dropped from out his trembling grasp, —
And at Time's feet his offerings lie.

Then knew I none could bear away the flower
That Time on each and all bestows ;
Nor would I take his gift when he
To me in turn held out a rose.

Eheu, fugaces, Posthume, Posthume, Labuntur Anni.

FLEETING years are ever bearing,
    In their silent course away,
All that in our pleasures sharing
    Lent to life a cheering ray.

Beauty's cheek but blooms to wither,
    Smiling hours but come to fly;
They are gone : Time 's but the giver
    Of whate'er is doomed to die.

Thou may'st touch with blighting finger
  All that sense can here enjoy;
Yet within my soul shall linger
  That which thou canst not destroy.

Love's sweet voice shall there awaken
  Joys that earth cannot impart:
Joys that live when thou hast taken
  All that here can charm the heart.

As the years come gliding by me,
  Fancy's pleasing visions rise;
Beauty's cheek, ah! still I see thee,
  Still your glances, soft blue eyes!

The World.

'T is all a great show
  The world that we 're in:
None can tell when 't was finished,
  None saw it begin;
Men wander and gaze through
  Its courts and its halls, —
Like children whose love is
  The picture-hung walls.

There are flowers in the meadow,
  There are clouds in the sky,
Songs pour from the woodland,
  The waters glide by: —

Too many, too many
   For eye or for ear,
The sights that we see
   And the sounds that we hear.

A weight as of slumber
   Comes down on the mind ;
So swift is Life's train
   To its objects we 're blind ;
I, myself, am but one
   In the fleet gliding show ;
Like others I walk,
   But know not where I go.

One saint to another
   I heard say, " How long? "
I listened, but nought more
   I heard of his song.
The shadows are walking
   Through city and plain
How long shall the night
   And its shadow remain ?

How long ere shall shine,
   In this glimmer of things,
The Light of which prophet
   In prophecy sings ;
And the gates of that city
   Be open, whose sun
No more to the west
   Its circuit shall run!

My Mother's Voice.

My mother's voice! I hear it now;
I feel her hand upon my brow,
   As when in heartfelt joy
She raised her evening hymn of praise,
And called down blessings on the days
   Of her loved boy.

My mother's voice! I hear it now;
Her hand is on my burning brow,
   As in that early hour
When fever throbbed through all my veins,
And that fond hand first soothed my pains
   With healing power.

My mother's voice! It sounds as when
She read to me of holy men,
   The Patriarchs of old :
And, gazing downward in my face,
She seemed each infant thought to trace
   My young eyes told.

It comes — when thoughts unhallowed throng,
Woven in sweet deceptive song,
   And whispers round my heart;
As when at eve it rose on high
10

I hear, and think that she is nigh,
    And they depart.

Though round my heart all, all beside,
The voice of Friendship, Love had died,
    That voice would linger there;
As when, soft pillowed on her breast,
Its tones first lulled my infant rest,
    Or rose in prayer.

Forevermore.

A SAD refrain I heard, from poet sad,
Which on my soul with deadening weight did
        fall;
But quick another word, which made me glad,
Did from the heavens above me seem to call.
The first was Nevermore; which, like a knell,
Struck on my ear with dull funereal sound;
The last was Evermore; which, like a bell,
In waves of music filled the air around.
Forevermore with loved and lost to be,
No more to suffer change, nor grief, nor pain;
From partings sad to be forever free, —
Such was that sweet bell's music: — its refrain
Blended with voices from the heavenly shore,
Each whispering to my heart, Forevermore.

The Beginning and the End.

The Word.

I.

WHAT is the word? I often hear men say,
Greeting each other in the mart or street;
Seeking for something new, from day to day,
Of friend or neighbor whom they chance to
      meet.
The question wakes in me the thoughtful mind;
Do they receive the word they ask to hear?
Or is it only like the passing wind,
Or empty echo dying on the ear?
The Word, O Man, is not some idle sound,
Lost on the ear almost as soon as heard:
Unto the wise life-giving it is found,
And by its voice the inmost soul is stirred:
It falls not on the ground a barren seed,
But springeth up in fruitful thought and deed.

II.

The voice that speaks when thou art in thy tomb,
And spoke before thou saw'st the morning light;
This is The Word! of all that is the womb,
Of all that see, the never-failing sight;
Speechless, yet ever speaking, none can hear
The man grown silent in the praise of God;

For they within Him live, to hope and fear;
They walk and speak; but He, — the grass-
    grown sod.
Its presence round them calls them forth to It,
A voice too great for murmur or reproof;
A sun that shines till they of It are lit,
Itself the utterance of Eternal Truth:
Perfect, without a blemish; never found
Save through the veil that wraps thy being
    round.

The Rock.

Thou art: there is no stay but in thy love;
Thy strength remains; it built the eternal hills;
It speaks the Word forever heard above,
And all creation with its presence fills;
Upon it let me stand, and I shall live;
Thy strength shall fasten me forever fixed,
And to my soul its sure foundations give,
When earth and sky thy Word in one has mixed.
Rooted in Thee no storm my branch shall tear,
But with each day new sap shall upward flow;
And still thy vine the clustering fruit shall bear,
That with each rain the lengthening shoots may
    grow,
Till o'er thy Rock its leaves spread far and wide,
And in its green embrace its Parent hide.

The Soldier.

He was not armed like those of eastern clime,
Whose heavy axes felled their heathen foe ;
Nor was he clad like those of later time,
Whose breast-worn cross betrayed no cross be-
      low ;
Nor was he of the tribe of Levi born,
Whose pompous rites proclaim how vain their
      prayer ;
Whose chilling words are heard at night and
      morn,
Who rend their robes, but still their hearts would
      spare.
But he nor steel nor sacred robe had on,
Yet went he forth in God's almighty power :
He spoke the Word whose will is ever done
From day's first dawn till earth's remotest hour ;
And mountains melted from his presence down,
And hell, affrighted, fled before his frown.

The War.

I saw a war : yet none the trumpet blew,
Nor in their hands the steel-wrought weapons
      bare ;
And in that conflict armed there fought but few,

And none that in the world's loud tumults share;
They fought against their wills, — the stubborn
     foe
That mail-clad warriors left unfought within,
And wordy champions left unslain below, —
The ravening wolf though drest in fleecy skin.
They fought for peace, — not that the world can
     give;
Whose tongue proclaims the war its hands have
     ceased,
And bids us as each other's neighbor live,
Ere haughty Self within us has deceased;
They fought for Him whose kingdom must in-
     crease,
Good will to men, on earth forever peace.

The Railroad.

Thou great proclaimer to the outward eye
Of what the Spirit, too, would seek to tell:
Onward thou go'st, appointed from on high
The other warnings of the Lord to swell.
Thou art the voice of one that through the world
Proclaims in startling tones, "Prepare the way;"
The lofty mountain from its seat is hurled,
The flinty rocks thine onward march obey;
The valleys, lifted from their lowly bed,
O'ertop the hills that on them frowned before;
Thou passest where the living seldom tread,

Through forests dark, where tides beneath thee
    roar ;
And bid'st man's dwelling from thy track re-
    move,
And would'st with warning voice his crooked
    paths reprove.

Love.

I ASKED of Time to tell me where was Love :
He pointed to her footsteps on the snow,
Where first the angel lighted from above,
And bid me note the way and onward go.
Through populous streets of cities spreading
    wide,
By lonely cottage rising on the moor,
Where bursts from sundered cliff the struggling
    tide,
To where it hails the sea with answering roar,
She led me on ; o'er mountain's frozen head,
Where mile on mile still stretches on the plain,
Then homeward whither first my feet she led,
I traced her path along the snow again ;
But there the sun had melted from the earth
The prints where first she trod, a child of mortal
    birth.

Thy Beauty Fades.

THY beauty fades, and with it, too, my love;
For 't was the self-same stock that bore its
     flower.
Soft fell the rain, and, breaking from above,
The sun looked out upon our nuptial hour;
And I had thought forever by thy side
With bursting buds of hope in youth to dwell,
But one by one Time strewed thy petals wide,
And every hope's wan look a grief can tell:
For I had thoughtless lived beneath his sway,
Who like a tyrant dealeth with us all,
Crowning each rose, though rooted on decay,
With charms that shall the Spirit's love enthrall,
And for a season turn the soul's pure eyes
From virtue's changeless bloom that time and
     death defies.

Beauty.

I GAZED upon thy face, — and beating life
Once stilled its sleepless pulses in my breast,
And every thought whose being was a strife
Each in its silent chamber sank to rest.
I was not, save it were a thought of thee;
The world was but a spot where thou hadst trod;

From every star thy glance seemed fixed on me;
Almost I loved thee better than my God.
And still I gaze, — but 't is a holier thought
Than that in which my spirit lived before,
Each star a purer ray of love has caught,
Earth wears a lovelier robe than then it wore,
And every lamp that burns around thy shrine
Is fed with fire whose fountain is divine.

The Hours.

THE minutes have their trusts as they go by,
To bear thy love who wings their viewless
    flight;
To Thee they bear their record as they fly,
And never from their ceaseless round alight.
Rich with the life Thou liv'st they come to me, —
Oh! may I all that life to others show;
That they from strife may rise and rest in Thee,
And all thy peace in Christ by me may know.
Then shall the morning call me from my rest,
With joyful hope that I thy child may live;
And when the evening comes, 't will make me
    blest
To know that Thou wilt peaceful slumbers give;
Such as Thou dost to weary laborers send,
Whose sleep from Thee doth with the dews de-
    scend.

The Beginning and the End.

Thou art the First and Last, the End of all
The wandering spirit seeks of earth to know;
Thee first it left, a Parent, at its fall;
To Thee again thy wilful child must go:
With awe I read the promise of thy grace,
To all that disobey so freely given;
The child shall see again his Father's face,
And   through   thy   love   return   to   Thee   and
        heaven.
Ye spirits that around your Maker stand,
Rejoice! the world is ransomed from its woe.
O earth! obey your Sovereign's wise command,
'T was He who bade for you his mercy flow;
It is for you his love descends like rain,
That you through Him may rise to life again.

Index of First Lines.

Printed in the USA
CPSIA information can be obtained
at www.ICGtesting.com
CBHW050714020124
3105CB00009B/948